747 THINGS TO DO ON A PLANE

From *Liftoff* to Landing, All You Need to Make Your Travels Fly By

JUSTIN CORD HAYES

adamsmedia

avon, massachusetts

To my son, Parker-John, with much love. May your journeys always be happy ones, and may you always return safely home from them.

Published by Adams Media, an F+W Publications Company
57 Littlefield Street, Avon, MA 02322. U.S.A.
www.adamsmedia.com

ISBN-13: 978-1-59869-541-0
ISBN-10: 1-59869-541-X
Printed in Canada.
J I H G F E D C B A
Library of Congress Cataloging-in-Publication Data is available from the publisher.

This publication is designed to provide accurate and authoritative information with regard to the subject matter covered. It is sold with the understanding that the publisher is not engaged in rendering legal, accounting, or other professional advice. If legal advice or other expert assistance is required, the services of a competent professional person should be sought.

    —From a *Declaration of Principles* jointly adopted by a Committee of the American Bar Association and a Committee of Publishers and Associations

Certain sections of this book deal with activities and devices that would be in violation of various federal, state, and local laws if actually carried out or constructed. F+W Publications, Inc., does not advocate the breaking of any law. This information is for entertainment purposes only. We are not responsible for, nor do we assume any liability for, damages resulting from the use of any information in this book.

Many of the designations used by manufacturers and sellers to distinguish their product are claimed as trademarks. Where those designations appear in this book and Adams Media was aware of a trademark claim, the designations have been printed with initial capital letters.

Contains material adapted and abridged from *The Everything® Pencil Puzzles Book*, by Charles Timmerman, copyright © 2006 by F+W Publications, Inc.; *The Everything® Brain Strain Book*, by Jake Olefsky, copyright © 2005 by F+W Publications, Inc.; and *The Everything® Lateral Thinking Puzzles Book*, by Nikki Katz, copyright © 2006 by F+W Publications, Inc.

Illustration on page iv © iStockPhoto / Janne Ahvo.

This book is available at quantity discounts for bulk purchases.
For information, please call 1-800-289-0963.

CONTENTS

ACKNOWLEDGMENTS

It's impossible to come up with so many ideas on your own. I offer 747 thank-yous to all my friends, family, and students who helped me come up with many of them.

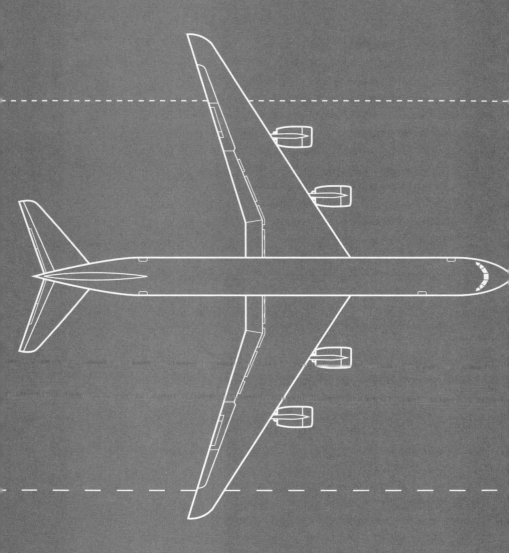

INTRODUCTION

Fewer than 100 years ago, human flight was so new that merely getting onto a plane and flying was magical. *Oh, how times have changed.* Now, flying is more of a hassle than an adventure. Elbowroom has shrunk virtually to nothing. The onboard meals are still bad—and now cost an arm and a leg. And any movies they show have been edited so as not to offend anyone.

Don't despair, though. There are actually many things you can do on a plane, and during those awful layovers. (Just reading this book being one of them!) Luckily for you, here's a list of activities to do and ideas to ponder, questions to ask seatmates and puzzles to fill in on your own, and plenty more ways to make your flying experience something to write home about.

So pack your bags. Get to the airport early, even though your flight is likely to be delayed. Endure those lengthy checkpoints. Stow that carry-on. Buckle up. Say a little prayer to the gods of flight. Then get ready to try out some of the 747 things you can do on a plane.

THE THINGS THAT NEVER GET DONE

There are so many distractions in your busy life that all the little things you intended to do just fall to the wayside and never get done. These small tasks could easily benefit your life; however, you just don't have the time to sit down and do them—until now. You're sitting, right? You've got some extra time on your hands, right? Then what are you waiting for? Dive in and do all the little things you never seem to have a chance to get to on the ground. Your to-do list will thank you.

1
Update your agenda.

Break out that trusty planner and start filling in dates with all the appointments, meetings, and special events that have yet to make their way to paper (or screen if you're out of the Stone Age and gone digital with a PDA, iPhone, or Black-Berry). This will end all the hemming and hawing that goes along with trying to plan a get-together with friends—and will help save you from cancellation fees from your dentist.

2
Clean out your purse or wallet.

It's one of those tasks you always *intend* to do. Do you really need those phone-number-covered scraps of paper since you updated your BlackBerry? And those pictures! Some of them are of people you haven't dated since the first Bush administration. Toss them out. Next, prioritize your cards. Make sure the ones you constantly use (ID, debit, credit, etc.) are up front and space-fillers like that gym card you never use are stuck in the back.

3
Balance your checkbook.

It's not fun, but it needs to be done. Is that cash going to your "party" account, or is it going to pay your bills, where it belongs? Get out that checkbook and balance the dang thing already! You may realize you have more money than you thought. When you're on the ground, it's far too easy to find excuses for procrastination.

If you're like most people—especially most men—you never, ever read instructions. You could be missing out on any number of cool features available on your new high-tech gadget. Bring instruction manuals with you and pore over them. You'll gain maximum enjoyment from your recent purchases.

4
Read instruction manuals.

One handy book most people never actually read until it's too late is their car's owner manual. It's there for a reason! Make sure to pack it in your carry-on next to your latest pop-fiction paperback. Then when it's time to read, make the smart choice and opt to better understand the workings of your vehicle rather than the vexing advances of a lovelorn protagonist.

5
Learn how your car works.

In this age of e-speak, writing thank-you notes has become a lost art. But taking the time to thank someone with a real, live, three-dimensional card is good for the soul. You've got time during your flight, so use it to personalize cards for all recent gift givers.

6
Fill out all those thank-you cards.

7

Wrap some gifts.

Short safety scissors are acceptable on planes, so put them to good use. If you're traveling home for Christmas or to someone's wedding, use your flight to wrap small gifts. You've got the time to make them beautiful and to personalize them for your loved ones.

8

Write down important phone numbers.

Yes, you have them stored in your cell or BlackBerry. But what would happen if—*gasp*—you lost your phone? Or it breaks? Or you unexpectedly run out of battery? How many numbers do you actually have memorized? Write down the most important ones on a slip of paper and put that in your wallet or purse. You can thank me later.

9

Devise a fire safety plan.

Perhaps you remember to replace your smoke detector batteries twice a year, but you probably don't have a safety plan. Devise one during your flight. Include escape routes for your family members. Make a note to buy new fire extinguishers and an escape ladder for the second floor. Determine a place to meet up after you've left the house. When you get home, laminate the plan and post it somewhere that is accessible to everyone.

Take some time to think of ways you can make your home safe from break-ins. For example, do you have a deadbolt on every door that leads in from outside? Do your windows lock securely? Do you leave a few lights on in the house when you're not there? Make a list of what you can do to protect your property and check off that list once you return home.

10
Burglarproof your house.

Before you buy that McMansion, consider remodeling your present house. Think about ways you can improve it. You could turn that two-car garage into a game room, or you could finish off that basement and turn it into an apartment and get some extra cash. Jot down the best ideas. Figure out which ones you might be able to do yourself.

11
Come up with remodeling ideas.

Ah, life goes on. Even when you're six miles in the air, you've got responsibilities back home, including mouths to feed. Go ahead and think about the staples you'll need upon your return home. Write a list of what you'll need the next time you stop by the grocery store. If you have a list, you're likely to save money because you won't buy unnecessary items.

12
Make your grocery list.

13
Create an acceptable household budget.

A budget seems like a prison, but it's actually quite freeing. Once you know what you spend on bills each month, you can determine how much to spend on fun. You don't have to have conscience pangs every time you make an unnecessary purchase, as long as you've budgeted for those extras that make life worth living. Use your time to fashion a livable budget, keeping in mind that cable, beer, and video games are *not* necessary expenses.

14
Consider debt consolidation.

If you have more than two maxed-out credit cards and a host of additional debts, make a plan to consolidate that debt. Many companies will combine your debts, allowing you to pay them off in monthly installments you can afford. Go on the Web and Google "debt-consolidation companies" prior to your flight. Print out the information, bring it with you, and study it on the plane.

15
End credit card enslavement.

If you're like most people, you've got three or more credit cards. Bring your statements with you. Analyze the purchases you've made. Which of them were necessary and which of them were impulse buys? Seeing that in black and white is a good first step toward weaning yourself off of the plastic. After you've analyzed your purchases, figure out how much you would need to save each month to pay off all your cards in three to five years.

If you're always running late, you need to rethink how you manage your time. Think about ways to streamline your most common tasks. For example, as you chew your cereal in the morning, go ahead and empty the dishwasher between bites while your mouth is full. If you write similar e-mails regularly, make up a template you can cut and paste. Looking at your usual routine and coming up with small timesavers like these will allow for more time to relax.

16

Develop time-management skills.

Go through your box of photos at home and pick out the ones you'd like to crop for an album. Bring along some safety scissors. Spend your flight cropping the photos. It goes without saying that you should not perform this activity during air turbulence, unless you have extra copies of the photos.

17

Crop photos for framing.

If your spare eyeglasses are broken or the lens on your sunglasses has come out, bring them and an eyeglass repair kit with you onto the plane. You've got some time, so you may as well do something constructive with it. Fix those glasses so you can use them once again.

18

Fix eyeglasses or sunglasses.

19
ID your keys.

Go through your key ring and see if you can identify all the keys on it. Consider putting the extraneous ones in a drawer. Once you have cut down on the number of keys, make each key unique and distinguishable. Pick up a set of multicolored rubber caps that will help with this task, or use colored paper and tape. By making your front door key distinguishable from your back door key, you'll cut down on the time it takes to fumble through them.

20
Tie some flies.

Fly fishing is an art not only because it brings you peace as you become one with nature, but because you actually have to tie the flies you use to corral nature. Many books on fly-tying exist. Pick one up, buy the basic materials you'll need, and spend your flight putting together some flies for your next fishing adventure.

21
Plan day trips.

Now that you have a minute to yourself up in the air, schedule some more time for you to take off from home. No matter where you live, you're likely to be within easy driving distance of a place filled with scenic beauty, historical significance, or possibilities for family fun. Plan out some day trips you can take once you return home.

There's something about Walt Disney's vision that continues to resonate in the world's consciousness. Disneyland in California and Florida's Walt Disney World continue to be the very definition of "dream vacation," especially for children. Gather materials about cost, accommodations, and travel arrangements, and use your flight to plan your family's next perfect vacation.

22
Plan a
Disney trip.

When was the last time you had a minute to do some catalog shopping? It's probably been a while. Whether you choose to check out the SkyMall catalog, with its expensive gadgets and gizmos, or bring a department store's catalog with you, undergo some retail therapy at 30,000 feet.

23
Flip through
a catalog.

This activity usually shares the five-minute period of coffee and cereal consumption before the carpool arrives, or it's relegated to a subway activity where space and lighting are not conducive to a proper read. Pick up your favorite periodical before you board, or ask the flight attendant what they have available, and sit back and really enjoy the newspaper again.

24
Read the
newspaper.

WRITING
EXERCISES

While the cabin of a 747 isn't a cabin in the woods or Papa's house in the Keys, it is a great place to write. You're isolated. You're focused. And you've got plenty of time to kill before touchdown. This chapter offers some writing exercises along with some writing goals, and it's sure to have you filling up the white space with ease—be it a few sheets of blank paper or a stack of cocktail napkins, whatever's handy.

25
Start the Great American Novel.

Surely you can produce something better than *Moby Dick*—it doesn't even have any car chases, gunfights, or sex scenes! And you have to wade through, like, seven hundred pages before you get to the final showdown between Captain Ahab and Moby Dick. How can Melville's tome be the Great American Novel? You've got hours to kill, so why not try your hand at literary immortality and debunk the white whale?

26
Write a screenplay.

Stop kvetching about that bad in-flight movie and *do* something about it. Surely you can come up with something better than yet another mindless special-effects extravaganza. Pick your favorite A-list actors and put them into a scenario of your own. By the time you're back on terra firma, you could be halfway to your first Oscar.

27
Write a one-act.

Who *really* needs the glitz and glamour of a major motion picture to tell a story? Heck, who even needs to change the scenery? A well-written one-act play provides suspense and humor in a short ten-minute package. Try your hand at making a script fit for the stage. Remember to include the stage directions and really milk the drama. If you think it's good enough, see if a local theatre group has any interest in performing it.

Mel Brooks's film *The Producers*—and the Broadway play based on it—centers on producers trying to create a musical they're sure will bomb. Their subject? Adolph Hitler. Try your own hand at creating the worst-ever musical. Pick a disgusting subject—garden slugs, flatulence, or Osama Bin Laden—and focus a musical on it. Write the basic plot. Write the words to some of the songs. Pick the actors and actresses you'd like to cast.

28
Write the world's worst musical.

He's not really a balding businessman who has fallen asleep over a crossword puzzle. He's the lover of that girl over there who's got a ring in her nose and a bored look on her face. She has poisoned him for getting it on with her lesbian lover, the middle-aged woman at the window seat who's got one of those sleep masks on. The possibilities for creating intrigue are endless!

29
Cast fellow passengers in a soap opera.

Most people cannot sing Francis Scott Key's "The Star Spangled Banner." The tune actually was created by a club devoted to drinking, which may explain the vocal gymnastics required to sing it. And the words, while uplifting, are related to an event that took place during the War of 1812. It's time for a facelift. Try your hand at a new national anthem. Just make sure it's something people can actually sing.

30
Write a new national anthem.

31
Write a country song.

Pull out every cliché you can about pickup trucks, tears, and hard-loving women. Arrange them in stanzas. Come up with a zippy chorus featuring a silly but impossible-to-forget rhyme like "achy" and "breaky." Voilà! You're on your way to Nashville's Ryman Auditorium and the Country Music Hall of Fame.

32
Write letters to your family.

Take your time onboard as a chance to really let your loved ones know how you feel. Write a letter from the heart to each of your immediate family members telling them what you appreciate about them, how much they've affected your life, and what, if any, boundaries stand between the two of you having a closer relationship. Mail them once you get off the plane.

33
Write apology letters.

All of us have done things we regret and have hurt people in our lives. Take responsibility for the part you have played in interpersonal Cold Wars. Write apology letters. Don't make excuses in them. Simply explain yourself as best you can and apologize for actions you realize now were wrong. Send them to the recipients as soon as you deplane, or read the letters to them over the phone.

Remember doing that? Back before cell phones, IMs, and e-mail, people actually wrote in pen on paper to catch up with their friends. It seems so old and antiquated now. But you can bring it back. People still get a great thrill from receiving something in the mail that isn't a bill or credit card offer. Brighten someone else's day by using your time above to write a letter and mail it once you land.

34
Write a letter just to say "Hi!"

Sometimes friendships end for no real reason. The two people just drift apart and it's easier to let the relationship peter out than keep it alive. Do something about that. Think of the last friendship you let fade away and write a letter to that person.

35
Write to a former friend.

"I never thought these letters were true until my trip to Aruba last year," begins a typical letter to the *Forum*. To this day, most folks believe that the racy and explicit epistles found in this adult magazine are, in fact, not true. They're fantasies. So dream a little. Make up your own letter. Claim its verity. Let your imagination go wild. Submit your fictional sexcapade to the magazine and see if they run it.

36
Write a letter to *Penthouse*'s *Forum*.

37
Write a "Dear Abby" letter.

Abigail Van Buren and her daughter who succeeded her have dispensed sage advice for the lovelorn and other sufferers since the 1950s. Folks send missives containing their ills to Abby, and in a few dozen words or so, she solves their problems. Surely you have some beef with life. Write down your biggest concern in a letter to "Abby," and send it in right away. And in no time—problem solved!

38
Dear diary ...

Self-understanding is a key to well-being. That's why folks throughout history have kept diaries of their daily lives. Use this time of miles-high reflection to start one yourself. Begin by jotting down generalities about recent events. Before long, you'll find yourself musing over what you've done and what you've failed to do in your life. You're likely to discover insights about yourself that you have not considered previously.

39
Write down a secret.

Ever visited *www.PostSecret.com*? People send in anonymous, creative postcards to the site that declare their deepest secrets for everyone to read. Do your own airline version. Use a napkin or blank piece of paper to illustrate your own secret-spilling postcard. Write down your deepest secret and then leave it in the in-flight magazine or plane's bathroom for someone else to find.

You may feel as if you're tempting fate, but what are the odds something will happen to your plane while you're actually writing your will? Most folks don't have a will, which means your family members may not get what you would like them to have. Since wills are complicated legal forms, use your time onboard to figure out how you want your assets distributed after you're gone. Then visit a lawyer and draft up the actual document once you land.

40
Make up your will.

Do you really want to leave an important chore like this up to your ex-wife or someone else who thinks you're Satan incarnate? Heck no! Besides, even loved ones will have an annoying tendency to stick close to the truth. Rewrite your life the way you think it should have been lived. Trumpet your nonexistent Pulitzer and Nobel prizes. Oh, and while you're at it, you can drop in that bit about curing cancer and the common cold.

41
Write your own (made-up) obituary.

Automatic writing is the process of emptying your mind and allowing the spirits of the dead to communicate through your pen or pencil. Get out a sheet of paper, place your writing instrument on it, and wait for the spirit to move you. If your contact with the spirits is successful, you'll have a piece of writing that is not in your style. Perhaps it will contain a message for you or for someone else.

42
Try automatic writing.

43

Make up neologisms.

Neologism is a fancy word meaning "new word." Neologisms seem to pop up daily in our always-evolving culture. Often they are designed to save time. A great neologism example is the word *blog*. What started as the term "web log" has evolved into the term blog, which can be used as a noun or a verb.

44

Can you make up a pangram?

A pangram is a sentence that contains all twenty-six letters of the alphabet at least once. The most famous is: The quick brown fox jumped over the lazy dog. All twenty-six letters, pretty impressive! Can you write down some more?

45

Create anagrams.

Anagrams are a fun way to boost your brainpower. Use all the letters in a person's name to form new words. Often, the results are hilarious or—at the very least—interesting. Here, for example, are some anagrams formed by the name George W. Bush: beg surge how, brew goes ugh, shrub egg woe. Take the name of a famous person and see how many you can make.

James Agee and Pauline Kael did their best to elevate film reviews to a high art, but hacks for Hollywood hire have done more than enough to make film "criticism" little more than jingoistic idiocy touting the worst dreck for the right price. Surely you can do better. Write your own reviews. Tell the truth. Don't pull your punches or withhold your praise. Then share these reviews with friends and coworkers or use them to start a blog.

46
Write book and film reviews.

Sonnets are a popular form of poetry, and they are challenging to write. The type Shakespeare wrote contains fourteen lines made up of three quatrains (sets of four lines) and a concluding, rhyming couplet. Each line is in iambic pentameter. An iamb is one unaccented syllable, followed by an accented syllable. "Pentameter" means there are five iambs in each line. The rhyme scheme is a-b-a-b, c-d-c-d, e-f-e-f, g-g. Good luck with this one!

47
Write a sonnet.

An acrostic is a sort of poetic puzzle. The first letter of each line, when read top to bottom spells out a word or name. Try to write an acrostic that can tell others about your personality and interests. You may even learn something about yourself.

48
Write an acrostic featuring your name.

49

Write a rap.

Some of today's best rap lyricists are on par with the world's best poets. Both types of writers strive for the same goal—a high impact of emotion through a rhythmic phrasing of words. Adopt your own rap persona while in the air and see if you can spit out sixteen bars, or lines.

50

A priest, a nun, and a rabbi ...

A standard convention for a joke, the priest, nun, and rabbi usually walk into a bar. Something inappropriate is almost always done. And a punch line is delivered that makes it obvious one of the holy trio is less pure than his or her drinking buddies. Working within those guidelines, see what kind of joke you can come up with. If you think it's funny enough, and your seatmate isn't easily offended, test out the joke.

51

Write a paragraph with no e's.

The letter e is the most prominent in the English language. It's everywhere! It's all over this very paragraph! Try to write a meaningful paragraph that does not contain a single e. It's not easy. It will take you some time, and it will get your creative juices flowing.

Think you can write a story that only uses nouns that are four letters long? It's a lot harder than you might think. First of all, your choice of character names is cut short, and so are the setting options and characters' occupations. Enjoy writing about Carl, the chef, and Lynn, the maid, who live in Ohio with their boys, Chip and Bill.

52
Write a story using only four-letter nouns.

We know, we know—you hated writing five-paragraph themes in high school. But you have to admit, they helped you organize your thoughts and synthesize ideas. These essays were the cornerstones for future activities such as planning meetings and writing business reports. Check to see if you still have those old skills. Pick a subject and write a five-paragraph theme about it.

53
Write a five-paragraph theme.

Children's books have become increasingly sophisticated in recent years. They seem to be written as much for adults as for kids. Try your hand at penning one. And these days, no topic is too outrageous to cover, so don't hold your imagination back!

54
Write a children's book.

55
Start an advice book for your children.

You've gained a certain amount of wisdom in your life, probably by virtue of learning from the mistakes you've made. Put your observations down on paper. Make them as foolproof to follow as possible. Then give the book to your kids. If you don't have children, go ahead and start your advice book anyway. You'll have a head start on the wisdom business once they're born.

56
Write a modern fairy tale.

If you look at them, you'll realize that your favorite childhood fairy tales were just warnings wrapped up in a plot and set in an enchanted forest. Little Red Riding Hood, for example, is about taking caution around strangers. The Three Little Pigs is about the steep price one can pay for doing things halfway. Make up your own set of modern tales, focusing on modern dilemmas, such as the perils of driving while talking on a cell phone.

57
Once upon a time ...

In stride with writing a modern-day fairy tale, you could also take a timeless classic and turn it on its head. Similar to what the 3-D wizards did in *Shrek*, you can use the stable of well-known fairy tale creatures to populate your own retelling of *Pinocchio* or *The Emperor's New Clothes*.

George Orwell's classic *Animal Farm* is an allegory for the British class system. In it, farm animals stand for members of the government and for people from the various strata of British society. Turn your focus on America, and write an allegory for the country's state of affairs.

58
Write a modern allegory.

Craft a short story where the protagonist is a member of your opposite sex. If you're a woman, really try to use your experience with men to get into the thought process of this male character. Understand that there are inherent differences between how he would speak or move because he is a man, and incorporate those details in your writing. If you're a man, good luck!

59
Write from the other gender's perspective.

No one knows your story better than you. Even if you've never done anything of earth-shattering importance, your loved ones would like to know more about you. Start with your earliest memories and hit every highlight you can recall. Who knows? You might even be able to publish your memoir. Such writers as Augusten Burroughs and Elizabeth Wurtzel have had their life-based writings turned into films.

60
Start an autobiography or memoir.

61
Write a story with a familiar character.

Take one of the great figures of the literary canon—Anna Karenina, Holden Caulfield, Jane Eyre, Jay Gatsby—and make him or her the protagonist of your own story. Put Jane Eyre into modern-day Manhattan. Take Holden Caulfield and place him in the Wild West. The possibilities are endless. How will you transform one of the world's great literary figures?

62
Rewrite the ending of a famous story.

Upset that Romeo and Juliet end up offing themselves? Or that the boys are rescued at the end of *Lord of the Flies*? Fix it! Rewrite the ending to Shakespeare's play so that the two star-crossed lovers end up escaping to Venice to open a *gelateria*. Or make it so the fire that the boys start actually catches the attention of *Lost*-style others who inhabit the island and not that of a passing warship. Have some fun and make the ending your own.

63
Make up dirty limericks.

All the menfolk in town went tut-tutty / At the lass who was known to be (fill in the blank). Even people who claim to hate poetry love dirty limericks. They're fun and clever. Put your skills to work. All you need to do is make up a good list of dirty words and double entendres, then you're all set. Have fun and set those Irish eyes to smilin'.

SPAM, which stands for SPiced Pork and hAM, first hit supermarket shelves in 1937. Since then, it's been both a national treasure and a national joke. Folks wonder just what's in that distinctive can. Then someone invented the SPAM-ku, a haiku centered on—what else—SPAM. A haiku is a Japanese form of poetry that contains three lines. The first line has five syllables, the second seven, and the third five. Try your hand at writing SPAM-kus.

64
Write a SPAM-ku.

A satire takes a particular author's patented prose and gives it a metaphorical pinch on the buttocks. Annual "bad Faulkner" and "bad Hemingway" contests exist, for example. Would-be Nobel Prize-winners ape the styles of these literary lions, and the results often are hilarious. Try your hand at aping your own favorite author. If she's still alive, send her the results. She'll probably get a kick out of your tribute.

65
Write a satire.

A roman à clef (pronounced roh-MAHN ah-CLAY) is a novel that focuses on real-life events with just enough fiction for the author to avoid libel. A recent example would be the novel *Primary Colors*, which fictionalized the Clinton presidency. Look at your own workplace and write a slightly fictionalized story about the drama and drudgery of a day in your office.

66
Start a roman à clef.

67
Write your own ballad.

If you've ever listened to the whole album of an '80s hair band, you've heard a ballad. Ballads tend to have frequent rhymes, a singsong pattern, and a recurring chorus. Most importantly, ballads tell stories. Think of your own life, and try to transform it into a ballad.

68
Write a Post-it story.

Get out a pack of Post-it notes. Write the first sentence of a story on it. Put the Post-it on your upright tray table. Then hand the Post-its to your neighbor. Ask her to add the next sentence. Then have her pass the pad to the guy with the window seat. Before long, you'll have a collaborative short story.

69
Write backward.

A simple way to boost your brainpower is to write sentences backward. By doing so, you force yourself to consider language from a new context because there's a sizeable difference between "I want to go home" and "Home go to want I." If you really want to make your head spin, try writing upside down and backward.

Come up with a crazy scenario and write out what you would do in response. Like say, a rhinoceros started charging your car ... how would you react to save your life? So what if you don't have any *real* survival skills. Make it up!

70
What would you do?

Flash fiction is an extremely short story. All the elements of a good story are there—characters, conflict, and resolution—however, it all happens within a single page (if that). Come up with a story arc and then write it as tight as possible. Then pare it down. Then pare it down again. And again. A lot of literary magazines and anthologies run special sections or issues of just flash fiction. If you think yours is good enough, submit it.

71
Write a piece of flash fiction.

TRAVELING WITH A LITTLE CO-PILOT

Whining, screaming, kicking the seats, running down the aisles, throwing food—why would they ever let kids on a plane? Unless, of course, they're your little angels. Here are some great ideas on how to entertain your children while flying, so your fellow passengers don't look to toss you from the plane during your layover in Phoenix. Flying also provides some quality time with you and your kids that they can't run away from.

72
Count shapes in the plane.

A great way to occupy a child is to have her look for shapes. Have her pick a number and then you pick a shape; then it's her job to find enough things in the plane that are that chosen shape. This version of "I Spy" helps them learn to both recognize shapes and count, and keeps them quietly entertained. It's a win-win situation.

73
Get a new perspective on cloud creativity.

When you were small, you probably spent time lying on your back, staring up at the clouds and imagining that they were animals, cars, or cartoon characters. Now that you're well above the clouds, revisit your cloud-gazing youth with your child. See how he interprets the cloud patterns as you cruise through the skies.

74
Stay within the lines.

Odds are, you haven't touched a coloring book in decades. Return to those carefree days of childhood by picking up a coloring book and having some fun with your kid. Go wild. Color trees purple and people green. Teach her how to stay within the lines but to have some fun with her coloring. It's a great bonding exercise and a surprisingly calming activity.

A great way to help your child learn how to draw is by tracing. So, grab a piece of paper and have her pick out a picture from a book, or even something in the in-flight magazine. Help her trace the outline of the picture and then fill in the details. Then have her try to redraw the picture without tracing it.

75
Trace your way through it.

If stick figures remain her forte no matter how many times she practices drawing freehand, you could help her make a collage instead. Cut or tear out pictures from the in-flight magazine and SkyMall catalog. Assemble them in new, interesting ways. Artists such as Jane Frank and John Walker have made a living doing this. Your kid could be next—next stop eBay!

76
Make a collage.

Ask the flight attendant for some extra straws with your drink. Then start twisting. Have your child name an animal and see if you can replicate it with the straws. Some suggestions will be a lot easier to complete than others, and most will require some imagination. Let's hope your kid's into snakes.

77
Make animals from straws.

78
Scare him silly.

One of the best ways to keep kids entertained is by frightening the pants off of them. Nothing keeps them quiet like a good scary story. Use your twisted imagination to concoct a wicked (but age-appropriate) tale that would get the Crypt Keeper shaking. See what terrors you can conjure up to keep your kid diverted.

79
Tell a fish story.

Make up the ultimate story about "the one that got away" and become a heroic angler in the eyes of your child. Throw in some huge waves and a sinking boat. Steal a page from Hemingway and make it a marlin you fought for three days before your line finally broke. Share it passionately with your pint-sized seatmate and watch her face light up.

80
Make shadow puppets.

If you're traveling at night and it's dark in the cabin, use your overhead light to make shadow puppets. Use your index and middle fingers as rabbit ears. Hook your thumbs and wave your hands to make a bird. Curl your middle and ring fingers and stick out your index finger and pinkie to create a bull. Experiment with other finger positions and help your little companion fill a shadowy zoo.

One way to calm the complaints of your TV-less child is to bring their favorite cartoon characters to life. Start responding to their questions as if you were Scooby-Doo. Tell them not to kick the seat in the same tone as Dora the Explorer. Help them order their meal in the voice of Sponge Bob. Sure, it's embarrassing, but nothing's too humiliating for your little angel.

81
Imitate cartoon characters.

Keep your little swashbuckler occupied by giving him a crash course in the salty speech of pirates. Have him answer in the affirmative with a hardy "Aye, matey" and refer to the parts of the plane as if it were a ship. Mix in lessons on creative grammar and syntax and soon his bathroom requests will come out like, "Aaahhrrr, me hearty, stern is where I be going to hit the head." Just be sure he knows pirate-speak is for the plane, not the classroom.

82
Aaahhrrr!

Whip out a comb and a piece of tissue paper and let your kid go at it with one humdinger of a twangy instrument. Simply have her put the tissue over the teeth of the comb, put the comb against her mouth, and *voilà*—instant musical instrument. Just beware of any passengers who might get to their last nerve with your mini-hillbilly.

83
Play the comb.

84
Sing some *Schoolhouse Rock.*

Educate your child with a catchy tune from this series of short educational "commercials" broadcast on ABC in the '70s. *Schoolhouse Rock* exposed kids to grammar, history, science, and math—and they loved it! Start singing a throwback like "I'm Just a Bill" or "Conjunction Junction" and watch how quickly it catches on.

85
Start a round.

A round is a song in which two or more people sing the same words but start at different times. The one you're most likely to be familiar with is "Row, Row, Row Your Boat." Start singing and when you get to the end of "gently down the stream," have your child begin with the "Row, row, row" part. See if you can get a round going. It's sure to cause some smiles as you race along in song.

86
Play with the food.

Let your kids put their airline food to good use—have them make some sculptures with whatever's left over. Give them a chance to be creative and have some fun doing something they know they wouldn't get away with at the dinner table. Just be sure they don't make a mess or fling any mashed potatoes at fellow passengers.

Make use of that airsickness bag by drawing eyes on it and giving it a nose and impish grin. Then stick your hand in the bag and move the bottom flap up and down in time with your speaking. Name your new creation and introduce it to your young seatmate. Jim Henson would be proud.

87
Put on a puppet show.

A great way to stave off your child's boredom during a lengthy flight is to buy several small, inexpensive toys and gift wrap them. Prepack them in your child's carry-on backpack and let her spend the flight unwrapping the gifts and playing with her new toys. When she gets bored with one, she can open another.

88
Entertain your child with presents.

It doesn't matter what time of year it is, kids are always considering what they'll be dressing up as next Halloween. Brainstorm a list of creative ideas. Get weird. Take chances. Once you've narrowed down the list to *the* costume, let him draw what he thinks it should look like.

89
Design a costume for next Halloween.

90
Picture fellow passengers as cartoon characters.

Let your child use his imagination and match up fellow passengers with some of his favorite fictional characters. It's a creative and fun exercise that will keep him entertained. Just be careful he doesn't call out to someone with an unflattering resemblance. Pointing at a woman and yelling "Porky Pig" probably isn't a safe bet for either of you.

91
Create a new cartoon character.

It's said that Walt Disney conceived of Mickey Mouse while riding a train. Disney's empire now stretches around the globe. Would Disney's cartoon creation have been different if conceived during a transatlantic flight? With the help of your kid, take a cue from Walt and use your time traveling as a brainstorming session for the next big animated superstar.

92
Create a children's show.

Those guys in *The Wiggles*, a children's show from Down Under, are among the richest people in Australia. You can't stand them, but your toddlers would probably stomp on your prone body to get to a real, live Wiggle. Put your head together with your child and see if you can come up with your own kids' show that will have you wiggling all the way to the bank.

Cartoonland is filled with a pantheon of heroes. Some are larger than life, while some are minuscule. Some screw up repeatedly before finally saving the day. And some just have one bad day after another. Find out which cartoon character your child would choose to be if she suddenly could become animated. Ask her why she chose that particular character. You can gain a lot of insight into your child's personality with a simple question.

93
I'd be Mighty Mouse.

Pick up an Etch A Sketch at a toy store before your flight, and use your time in the air to challenge your mini-me to a knob-off. Choose something to render in aluminum powder and then each of you take a timed chance at illustrating it on the Etch A Sketch the best. Get an objective third party to judge your designs, and try not to showboat too much when you leave your six-year-old in your knob-twirling dust.

94
Extend an Etch A Sketch duel.

Help your child write his seasonal list of wants to Old Saint Nick. It doesn't matter what time of the year it is, a kid is always happy to tell you all the new toys he wants. See if he'll include a good word for you in his letter, and then mail it off to the North Pole once you land.

95
Write a letter to Santa.

96
Play with some Hot Wheels.

Hot Wheels are those toy cars that boys have been collecting and trading for years. The little roadsters still exist, and they're just as much fun to roll around as they ever were. Bring some with you and hold a race on your tray table.

97
Play with Mr. Potato Head.

When Mr. Potato Head arrived in 1952, he was—literally—meant for potatoes. All you got was various facial features that you stuck into a spud. By 1960, he was given a large plastic potato body to go along with his various parts. Since then, he's also gained a wife and many different accoutrements. Stick him and all his pieces in your carry-on and have some fun with your daughter making a Picasso Potato.

98
Play with action figures.

Your youngster is sure to have packed some action figures in his tiny carry-on. Have him pull them out so the two of you can play with them together. You don't necessarily have to make the figurines fight. Instead, try something inventive. Put GI Joe in the middle of *Romeo and Juliet* and have him act out a few Shakespearean scenes (with your help, of course).

You've got instant inspiration! Bring some paper with you and help your child experiment with different methods of construction: short wings, sleek wings, sharp noses, blunt noses. Take bets as to which of the paper fliers will make it the farthest and then put them to the test once you deplane.

99
Make paper airplanes.

Remember Silly Putty? It's that elastic stuff you embedded in your folks' carpet and chucked at their walls. Put it to less destructive but equally fun uses as you cruise through the sky. Have your child press it against some newspaper, or fashion it into a ministatue.

100
Play with Silly Putty.

An advertising campaign once touted the unsinkable quality of the breakfast cereal, Cheerios. Just like little life preservers, the tiny Os just won't sink in milk. Put them to the test. Ask the flight attendant for a bowl and see if you and your little compatriot can prove the General Mills ad people wrong.

101
Sink Cheerios.

102
Put together a Snaptite model.

Snaptite models require no rubber cement. Just find the right pieces, fit them together, and they snap into place. The decals are easy to affix as well. Kits are available at toyshops and department stores, and they are a great diversion for little idle hands.

103
Decorate a T-shirt.

Pack a plain white t-shirt in your carry-on along with some markers and other art supplies that will help make a great fashion statement. Break them out and set up a traveling design studio for your little Armani-in-the-making. Give him free reign as to how he wants to style his shirt.

104
Make bookmarks.

Visit a craft supply store and pick up some card stock and markers. Then put your safety scissors to good use. Cut up the card stock into rectangles suitable for use as bookmarks and let your little bookworm spend the flight decorating the bookmarks. She can use them herself or give them out to all her friends.

Pick up toy tops before you get on the plane and turn your tray table into a battle arena. Face off against your kid in a mile-high top match. If you didn't grab a few tops before the trip, break out quarters and teach your child how to spin Washington. Once he's gotten the hang of it, see whose quarter will be triumphant in a spin-off. The point goes to whoever's quarter knocks the other one's down, or whoever's quarter spins the longest.

105
Battle tops.

Challenge your little seatmate to a spell off. Come up with grade-appropriate words and put her to the test. Let her ask for a sentence, origin, and pronunciation as if it were the real thing. And give her the chance to try and stump you by coming up with words for you to spell.

106
Hold a spelling bee.

A lot of kids have trouble pronouncing words and speaking clearly. Put an early end to this by using your flight time to help your child practice speaking. Pick up the in-flight magazine and have him quietly read a few sentences from an article out loud. Whenever he struggles with a word or does not enunciate it correctly, politely stop him, say the word, and have him repeat it. He'll be ready for broadcast news in no time.

107
E-*nun*-ci-ate clearly.

108
Study for a test.

As a parent, you know it's important for children to study for every test. As a former student, you know how much it sucked to study for tests. Use this time on board to go over any subjects your child needs to study. There aren't as many distractions as there are at home, and if you make it fun and easygoing, you both may end up having a good time.

109
Make up a country.

Let your miniature monarch create her own country. Let her give it a form of government, draw a map for it, and label her new country's major geographical features: rivers, lakes, mountain ranges, and so on. Help her decide who founded the country and any major historical events it had to go through. This exercise in creativity is a great way to help your kids learn about geography, civics, and history.

110
Design your own coat of arms.

A great example of family heritage is the coat of arms. These storied representations of a family's history can be emblazoned on just about anything. Give your child a chance to make history and come up with your own coat of arms. Draw the outline of a shield on a blank piece of paper and then let him go to town filling it in with things that he thinks represent your family.

It's probably been a while since you went through all your times tables, so take this as an opportunity to refresh your math skills and drop some knowledge on your tot. Teach her how to recite the times tables, and by the time you land, you'll have a math genius in the making.

111
Review the times tables.

Hand your child the in-flight magazine and a pen. Have her circle verbs, underline nouns, and put a box around adjectives. Time him and make it a race. Kids love races and parents love learning.

112
Identify parts of speech.

Engage your small-fry seatmate in conversation. There can be a lot of wisdom in little minds, and you get to sound like an expert on virtually everything because of your greater experience.

113
Talk to a child.

114
Level with your teenager.

If you're sharing an eight-hour flight with your teenage son or daughter, the experience doesn't have to be torturous. Take some time to level with your child about mistakes you've made in your life and about the lessons you've learned. Don't try to be perfect. Your teenager may respond in kind, and you'll connect in ways you didn't think possible.

115
Compare child-raising tips.

Chances are your kid won't be the only one on your flight. So more than likely you'll be in the vicinity of another parent. Take the time when your child goes down for a nap to chat with this comrade in parental arms. Trade war stories from battles past and techniques you may want to use in future conflicts.

COUNT
PASSENGERS

Oh, the joy of people watching. It's one of society's favorite hobbies and probably something you do every day, whether or not you're six miles up. But an airplane is the perfect place to people watch—so take advantage. Within this chapter, I've outlined a couple dozen of the best kinds of people to spot. So do a lap around the plane and count up how many of each you can spot. Keep track of the totals and see if you can best yourself on the return trip and future flights. It's like a safari, without the head mounting.

116
Count the business travelers.

A professional en route to a business meeting is an easy one to spot: suit, expensive watch, BlackBerry, pained look as if she's willing the plane to speed up. You may need to sweet talk your way up to the business-class section to get a higher head count. **TOTAL:** _____

117
Count multitaskers.

Easily thought of as synonymous with the business traveler, the two are not mutually exclusive. All multitaskers are not businesspeople and all businesspeople are not always multitasking. Look for anyone doing more than one thing at a time, like reading and feeding a baby, watching the in-flight movie and writing, or eating and holding a conversation—manners and multitasking are not mutually exclusive either. **TOTAL:** _____

118
Count air marshals.

Most flights would only have one air marshal on board, if any. However, she will be incognito as she keeps an eye on passenger safety. So part of this count is figuring out who she is. Look for someone who's fit, has a holster bulge, and is actually interested in looking you in the eye. **TOTAL:** _____

Okay, it's never good to assume the worst, but do it for a second. You've seen *Alive*; you know what I'm talking about! If the plane were to make a crash landing, whom would you eat? Don't necessarily opt for the fat guy—he's probably full of toxins. You want people who have a tone to their body, but enough meat on their bones where it'd be worth the awkward conversation. Think: former NFL player. **TOTAL:** _____

119
Count potential meals.

Which of your fellow passengers are coasting down Joan Rivers Highway with a few too many nips, tucks, and pricks? Check out their facial features for telltale signs like unnaturally tight skin, unmoving brows, overly puffy top lips, tiny nose bridges, or a face that looks like it's been caught in a permanent wind tunnel. **TOTAL:** _____

120
Count bad cosmetic surgery.

As hip as it's becoming to be a geek, the true breed are as easy to spot as a white guy at a Roots concert. Classic signs like thick glasses, greased combovers, and pocket protectors aren't typically de rigueur now, but *Star Wars* novels, pasty skin, and an air of social awkwardness are usually good indications. **TOTAL:** _____

121
Count geeks.

122
Count Eurotrash.

These are folks who suffer dramatically from ennui and attempts at oversophistication. Their look involves a lot of hair gel, tight clothes, big sunglasses, and Armani—for both the men and women. **TOTAL:** _____

123
Count the drunks.

Some people pregame too hard at the airport bar before boarding, and others enjoy one too many cocktails in the cabin. Either way, a drunk at 30,000 feet is just as funny as his ground brethren, only a little loopier due to the pressure difference—just as long as he's not overly offensive or touchy-feely. You might check for them at the start of the flight and then circle back toward the end to see how many people got their in-flight drink on. **TOTAL:** _____

124
Count novice travelers.

These people are easy to spot—as long as you're not one. You'll have noticed them at your gate before you boarded. They were sitting close to the desk and had probably been there for an hour. Now on board, they look frightened to move and listen intently whenever the captain comes over the intercom, and actually believe that you'll only be waiting to taxi for a few minutes. **TOTAL:** _____

Easy to spot because he's probably wearing his sister's jeans, the hipster male completes his outfit with a tight T-shirt and an ironic accessory, like a plastic watch or slap-bracelet. His hipster girlfriend is probably wearing an outfit that's one part Punky Brewster, one part '80s Madonna, and one part GAP (but don't tell anybody). They will both have a look of disdain when the flight attendant tells them they don't serve PBR. **TOTAL:** _____

125
Count hipsters.

While the men and women serving our nation deserve to be sitting first class, they're probably riding coach with you. You can pick them out: They're most likely dressed in fatigues, have good posture, and are enjoying the airline food, as it's a step up from the mess hall. **TOTAL:** _____

126
Count service people.

Saturday Night Live alum Julia Sweeney used to play a character named Pat. His/her gender was questionable, and that was the focus of each Pat segment. As you're people watching, count the number of gender-ambiguous "Pats" you see. **TOTAL:** _____

127
Count "Pats."

128
Count animal look-alikes.

Every now and then you see a person that helps you believe all creatures came from the same place. He might have a nose like a pig or she may have a bulldog's jowls. Whatever way the resemblance strikes you, appreciate it as a sign that we are a part of the animal kingdom. TOTAL: _____

129
Count celebrity look-alikes.

As you do your lap around the plane, see if you do any double-takes. Some people have been blessed with the same look as Angelina Jolie, others look like Steve Buscemi—either way, they look like someone who should be riding first class or in a private jet. Just be careful if you notice a reality star look-alike in coach, it might actually be that person. TOTAL: _____

130
Count celebrity "if they were" look-alikes.

While a few people are blessed with the similar look of A-listers, some have the distinction of resembling a distorted version of a famous face. She looks like Conan O'Brien, if he were a woman. He looks like Don Cheadle, if he were Asian. Use your imagination. TOTAL: _____

They were first in line to board the plane, sprinted down the connector, were the first to put their bags in the overhead, and even walk with authority to the bathroom. They will also blow by the elderly and children when your plane lands. They're probably a big deal. **TOTAL:** _____

131
Count people in a constant rush.

There are people who just have *it*. They're interestingly unique, but genuine. Then there are those who don't have *it*, but try *really* hard to fake *it*. It doesn't matter what their end goal is, as their attempt to achieve it is so desperate it's obvious. **TOTAL:** _____

132
Count people who are trying too hard.

Frigid, stark, and unnerving may be one way to describe a New England winter; it's also a good description of most members of the six Northeastern states that make up the region. They'll make eye contact, but it will usually be right through you. If they warm up to you, however, it's a completely different story. Hit on a few key discussion points—foliage, the Red Sox, or the Kennedys—and it'll be like you're one of their own. **TOTAL:** _____

133
Count New Englanders.

134
Count slobs.

Do you even need a description? These are the people you dread getting placed next to in the random world of seat assignments. Their hair's unkempt; they've got stains on their clothes; and you and the rest of the cabin will be lucky if they hopped in the shower and threw on some deodorant before heading to the airport.

TOTAL: _____

135
Count honey-mooners.

You may be able to distinguish two faces if they ever stop fawning all over each other. Usually PDA like this in such a tight space is unwarranted and should be an arrestable offense. However, they just got married, so you have to let it slide.

TOTAL: _____

136
Count golden-agers.

These are those charming older couples who seem like they've been together since the beginning of time. He knows where to place her travel pillow and she knows when to ask the flight attendant for a Tom Collins so he can take his pills.

TOTAL: _____

The nicely trimmed front of this haircut says business class, while the wild back end says party on in coach. A relic of the '80s, it still pops up in places across the country. Sometimes meant as a joke, sometimes the real deal, don't discount any mullet—as it's a symbol of a good time. **TOTAL:** _____

137
Count mullets.

These girls (and occasionally guys) have that weird brownish-orange hue to them due to excessive trips to the tanning bed and nightly rituals of slathering on self-tanner. Most will also be unnaturally thin, like that scraggily french fry that got left under the heat lamp for too long. **TOTAL:** _____

138
Count tanorexics.

Young, urban professionals—it pretty much says it all. They look like they should be graduating from high school, but have clothes and a carry-on that probably cost close to a month's rent. If your destination isn't a metropolitan area, you may have caught the Yuppie on a rare trip to its location of origin. **TOTAL:** _____

139
Count Yuppies.

140

Count single parents.

Frazzled and on-edge with eyes constantly darting from baby to toddler to tween is probably the best way to spot a single parent. They need at least half a dozen sets of eyes to keep up with everything that's going on as they go it alone. **TOTAL:** _____

141

Count trendsetters.

You probably think they look ridiculous, but they're actually in the mode. It would be pointless to give you a specific trend to list, as it would be outdated and ridiculous (see next entry) before the ink even dries on the paper. You'll recognize trendsetters because they carry themselves with a confidence reserved only for those on the cutting edge of fashion—and they'll probably be sitting in first class. **TOTAL:** _____

142

Count outdated trendsetters.

The latest fashion trends are constantly changing, and you need to be on the ball if you're going to play the trend game. While some trends just look ridiculous, it's people who are a few minutes too late (we're talking to you, Crocs) or even hours past the trendsetting (don't laugh too hard at Crocs, Uggs) who end up looking the most ridiculous. See how many people sporting an outdated trend you can find. **TOTAL:** _____

A rare breed of young people that is gaining in population around college towns, the trustafarian is one part trust fund baby and one part Rastafarian. They're all about peace, love, pot, and damming the man, but drive around in brand new Audis with padded bank accounts to purchase plenty of petrulli and beeswax for their sweet dreads. **TOTAL:** _____

143
Count trustafarians.

Now that you know the players, make a game out of it. Draw out a five-by-five bingo board. Fill in the center square as a freebie. At random, place the different types of passengers in the remaining twenty-four squares. Find a fellow bingo enthusiast to play. Call out—*quietly*—when you spot a type of passenger and, if all agree to him or her filling the profile, mark that type off on your card. The first to create a horizontal, vertical, or diagonal line of five wins. **TOTAL:** _____

144
Play passenger bingo.

ANAGRAMMAR

Put your brain to the test as you soar through the sky with these puzzles that see if you can spot anagrams within a sentence to fill its grammatical hole. Use your mile-high advantage to pick out the word, rearrange the letters, and then fill in the blank. If you're nice enough, your seatmate will probably help you out with any that really throw you for a loop.

145
Anagrammar Puzzle #1

The jackhammers began tearing down the _____ walls of Pennsylvania Station.

ANSWER: _____

146
Anagrammar Puzzle #2

The king failed to notice the _____ that was already sitting on his throne.

ANSWER: _____

147
Anagrammar Puzzle #3

My cat Ryan likes to play with _____.

ANSWER: _____

148
Anagrammar Puzzle #4

Scan the _____ to find the peaches with the cheapest price.

ANSWER: _____

149
Anagrammar Puzzle #5

Except for the snakes, there was no danger in the _____.

ANSWER: _____

Is the _____ signed by one of your pupils?

ANSWER: _____

150
Anagrammar
Puzzle #6

Based on his height, the boy was ranked _____ in the gym class.

ANSWER: _____

151
Anagrammar
Puzzle #7

Francis _____ to solve puzzles like this one.

ANSWER: _____

152
Anagrammar
Puzzle #8

The coroner examined the _____ who was found in the nightclub's alley.

ANSWER: _____

153
Anagrammar
Puzzle #9

The _____ shall be painted pink before Monday.

ANSWER: _____

154
Anagrammar
Puzzle #10

155
Anagrammar Puzzle #11

The _____ had muscles from years of unloading freight at the docks.

ANSWER: _____

156
Anagrammar Puzzle #12

_____ was the capital of Japan before Tokyo.

ANSWER: _____

157
Anagrammar Puzzle #13

The smoothie had sour grapes, lemon, yogurt, and _____.

ANSWER: _____

158
Anagrammar Puzzle #14

She took eight pairs of shoes for her trip to _____.

ANSWER: _____

159
Anagrammar Puzzle #15

Each tone in the song could also be called a _____.

ANSWER: _____

As he was _____, he had the feeling that he was being followed.

ANSWER: _____

160
Anagrammar
Puzzle #16

The artist had to move the _____ when the studio's lease was cancelled.

ANSWER: _____

161
Anagrammar
Puzzle #17

The pastel parasols provided shade for their _____.

ANSWER: _____

162
Anagrammar
Puzzle #18

A cheap _____ is far better for you than a candy bar.

ANSWER: _____

163
Anagrammar
Puzzle #19

Her face had a big grin when he gave her the _____.

ANSWER: _____

164
Anagrammar
Puzzle #20

165
Anagrammar Puzzle #21

There is a remote chance that the _____ will destroy all life on Earth.

ANSWER: _____

166
Anagrammar Puzzle #22

Be sure to restock the _____ before the Fourth of July.

ANSWER: _____

167
Anagrammar Puzzle #23

Does anyone know what causes those _____ to be so hot?

ANSWER: _____

168
Anagrammar Puzzle #24

The _____ acted as if the officer had not seen him in the saloon.

ANSWER: _____

169
Anagrammar Puzzle #25

The poet wrote a terse note about the lack of _____ on the island.

ANSWER: _____

LETTER EQUATIONS

Who would have thought numbers and words could live together in such a harmonious, puzzling world? Letter equations are well-known phrases or facts that have been disguised by replacing key words with the first letter of each word. For example, "12 = I in a F" is the letter equation for "12 Inches in a Foot." Wrestle with these word/number tag-team puzzles as you fly through the skies. (The answers are on page 265 if a particular puzzle pins you.)

170
Letter Equation #1

12 = M in a Y

ANSWER: _____

171
Letter Equation #2

6 = P on a P T

ANSWER: _____

172
Letter Equation #3

12 = M on the M

ANSWER: _____

173
Letter Equation #4

1 = P of P P that P P P

ANSWER: _____

174
Letter Equation #5

13 = C in a S

ANSWER: _____

21 = D on a D

ANSWER: _____

175
Letter Equation
#6

24 = L in the G A

ANSWER: _____

176
Letter Equation
#7

1,000 = W a P is W

ANSWER: _____

177
Letter Equation
#8

26.2 = M in a M

ANSWER: _____

178
Letter Equation
#9

5 = R on the O F

ANSWER: _____

179
Letter Equation
#10

180
Letter Equation
#11

99 = B of B on the W

ANSWER: _____

181
Letter Equation
#12

5 = S on the C F

ANSWER: _____

182
Letter Equation
#13

100 = Z in a G

ANSWER: _____

183
Letter Equation
#14

60 = MPH that a C can R

ANSWER: _____

184
Letter Equation
#15

9 = P on a B F

ANSWER: _____

2 = T D and a P in a P T

ANSWER: _____

185
Letter Equation
#16

---

88 = K on a P

ANSWER: _____

186
Letter Equation
#17

---

2 = S on a T B

ANSWER: _____

187
Letter Equation
#18

---

3 = L K that L T M

ANSWER: _____

188
Letter Equation
#19

---

20 = F and T on the H B

ANSWER: _____

189
Letter Equation
#20

190
Letter Equation
#21

I C L Y = 354 D

ANSWER: _____

191
Letter Equation
#22

9 = S in T T T

ANSWER: _____

192
Letter Equation
#23

10 = E in a D

ANSWER: _____

193
Letter Equation
#24

3 = P C in the C W

ANSWER: _____

194
Letter Equation
#25

100 = D in a M

ANSWER: _____

23 = P of C in the H B

ANSWER: _____

195
Letter Equation
#26

384,400 K = the D to the M from the E

ANSWER: _____

196
Letter Equation
#27

2 = L in a P of P

ANSWER: _____

197
Letter Equation
#28

4 = Q in a W

ANSWER: _____

198
Letter Equation
#29

2 = Y between the S O and the W O

ANSWER: _____

199
Letter Equation
#30

PENCIL SURGERY

You don't need to worry about stowing away a scalpel to have some fun with these puzzles—a pencil will do just fine. What you need to do to fly through this section is follow the directions and cut a letter from one word—be it at the beginning, middle, or end—in order to make another word. Simple! A slice here, a cut there, and you'll be burning up the minutes left until your destination.

200
Pencil Surgery
Puzzle #1

Cut the last letter from a fold and get an earnest request.

ANSWER: _____ & _____

201
Pencil Surgery
Puzzle #2

Cut the middle one from this prime less than 200 and get a fearsome number.

ANSWER: ____._____ & _____

202
Pencil Surgery
Puzzle #3

Cut a middle letter while sitting behind the wheel and end up all wet.

ANSWER: _____ & _____

203
Pencil Surgery
Puzzle #4

Cut the first letter from a handy covering and make the world go round.

ANSWER: _____ & _____

204
Pencil Surgery
Puzzle #5

Cut the lowest digit from the Fahrenheit boiling point and get a jack with an ace.

ANSWER: _____ & _____

205
Pencil Surgery
Puzzle #6

Cut the first letter from what is under a hat and get the sky.

ANSWER: _____ & _____

Cut a middle letter from the ground and get a youth.

ANSWER: _____ & _____

206
Pencil Surgery
Puzzle #7

Cut the first letter from a month and get a curve.

ANSWER: _____ & _____

207
Pencil Surgery
Puzzle #8

Cut a middle letter from turmoil and get a tale.

ANSWER: _____ & _____

208
Pencil Surgery
Puzzle #9

Cut a middle digit from the second year of a century and get a quantity of dogs.

ANSWER: _____ & _____

209
Pencil Surgery
Puzzle #10

Cut the first letter when finding fault and catch a fever.

ANSWER: _____ & _____

210
Pencil Surgery
Puzzle #11

Cut the first letter from a new spouse and get carried away.

ANSWER: _____ & _____

211
Pencil Surgery
Puzzle #12

212
Pencil Surgery
Puzzle #13

Cut the first letter from a boat and become fashionable.

ANSWER: _____ & _____

213
Pencil Surgery
Puzzle #14

Cut the last letter from an evergreen and get the point.

ANSWER: _____ & _____

214
Pencil Surgery
Puzzle #15

Cut a middle letter from a journey and get a waiter's wage.

ANSWER: _____ & _____

215
Pencil Surgery
Puzzle #16

Cut a middle letter from the seashore and find out the expense.

ANSWER: _____ & _____

216
Pencil Surgery
Puzzle #17

Cut the highest digit from a teen integer^2 and get the result of a single digit^2.

ANSWER: _____ & _____

217
Pencil Surgery
Puzzle #18

Cut the first letter from where lawns grow and get a shape.

ANSWER: _____ & _____

Cut a middle digit from the number of seconds in a week and get a millennium.

ANSWER: _____ & _____

218
Pencil Surgery
Puzzle #19

Cut the last letter from this bean and get two cups.

ANSWER: _____ & _____

219
Pencil Surgery
Puzzle #20

Cut the first letter from a squeeze and get a twelfth.

ANSWER: _____ & _____

220
Pencil Surgery
Puzzle #21

Cut a middle letter from perspiration and get a place to sit.

ANSWER: _____ & _____

221
Pencil Surgery
Puzzle #22

Cut the last letter from a sad cut and get a refreshment.

ANSWER: _____ & _____

222
Pencil Surgery
Puzzle #23

Cut a middle letter from a computer input device and get a source of inspiration.

ANSWER: _____ & _____

223
Pencil Surgery
Puzzle #24

224
Pencil Surgery
Puzzle #25

Cut the last letter from two performers and get what's coming to you.

ANSWER: _____ & _____

225
Pencil Surgery
Puzzle #26

Cut a middle letter from Santa's address and get the man who quoted a black bird.

ANSWER: _____ & _____

226
Pencil Surgery
Puzzle #27

Cut the last digit from this many leagues and get a movie about caped Spartans.

ANSWER: _____ & _____

227
Pencil Surgery
Puzzle #28

Cut the last letter from where a teen performs a chore and get what a teen breaks.

ANSWER: _____ & _____

228
Pencil Surgery
Puzzle #29

Cut the first letter from a French dish's ingredient and get the last thing put in a coffin.

ANSWER: _____ & _____

229
Pencil Surgery
Puzzle #30

Cut a middle letter and turn this extraordinary residence into just another location.

ANSWER: _____ & _____

Cut the first letter from this banner and you'll fall behind.

ANSWER: _____ & _____

230
Pencil Surgery
Puzzle #31

Cut a letter from a food prep step and get something that puts a spring in your step.

ANSWER: _____ & _____

231
Pencil Surgery
Puzzle #32

Cut the first letter from the flame and you'll get something very angry.

ANSWER: _____ & _____

232
Pencil Surgery
Puzzle #33

Cut the first letter from this kind word and get something very cold.

ANSWER: _____ & _____

233
Pencil Surgery
Puzzle #34

Cut a letter from some ground growths and get something you put on your legs.

ANSWER: _____ & _____

234
Pencil Surgery
Puzzle #35

Cut a letter from this broken pane and you'll find it very difficult.

ANSWER: _____ & _____

235
Pencil Surgery
Puzzle #36

IF YOU'RE NEXT TO ...

This is your chance. When else will you have the opportunity to get free advice from a professional in a particular field? If you're sitting next to an authority on a specific matter, milk it for what it's worth. Don't piss them off, but milk it. You don't know this person and will most likely never see them again—unless, of course, you happen to be sitting next to a friend or relative—so relax your inhibitions and start asking questions until you have all your answers ... or the person next to you flags down the flight attendant and asks for a seat change.

236

If you're next to a fortune-teller ...

Plan your future. You can't get somewhere if you don't know where you're going. See if you can sweet-talk him or her into giving you a free reading, be it tarot cards, your palm, or just a good ol' fashioned crystal ball reading. See where she thinks you're headed in your professional and romantic life.

237

If you're next to a funeral director ...

Plan your funeral. Most folks don't want to think about the inevitable, but you will leave your loved ones grieving even more if you don't have all the plans in place for your funeral. Get some ideas on how to have a tasteful funeral. And see if he has any ideas on how to keep it under a budget so you don't leave your loved ones with extra debt.

238

If you're next to newlyweds ...

Give them some advice. If you've been happily married for decades, you must have some secrets for a healthy, happy marriage. If you're sharing your aisle with newlyweds, don't keep those good ideas to yourself. Give them advice: what to do, what not to do, when to do things, when not to do things. If you're not flying with newlyweds, you can still write down your ideas and give them to your children when they decide to tie the knot.

Ask them what the secret to a happy marriage is. If you find yourself sharing an aisle with a happily married couple, don't be afraid to quiz the happy pair about what has made their marriage so successful. Whether you're single or married, you can pick up pointers that you can use now or in the future.

239
If you're next to a happily married couple ...

Vent. Some people are just natural listeners. Feel out the person sitting next to you and see if he's receptive to your complaining. If he is, let it all out. Sometimes all you need is a sympathetic ear. Open up and tell him everything!

240
If you're next to an open ear ...

See what she's up to now. It's probably been years since you've last seen each other, so take this chance encounter to play catchup. See what other classmates are doing. Did that mouth-breather with the really bad acne ever clean up his act? Did those "perfect girls" ever get handed some hard knocks? Talk to your former classmate–current seatmate about everyone—just like you were in high school again.

241
If you're next to an old classmate ...

242

If you're next to someone who seems familiar ...

Try and figure out how you know her. Don't stare! But try and pick up a few prominent facial features and then cycle through all the people you've ever met. It could be a former coworker, or a childhood neighbor, or it could just be a stranger.

243

If you're next to a film buff ...

Try dueling film quotes. State a line from a movie and see if your seatmate can guess the flick. Then see if your seatmate can stump you. A variation is to offer a line of dialogue and see if your seatmate can come up with the next line.

244

If you're next to a rocksnob ...

See what's acceptable to listen to. Rock-snobs only listen to the best of the best, and they'll enter into any argument they can act as authority on. They'll correct anyone who says the Beatles were the best British Invasion band and counter with the fact that the Kinks were by far the fab four's superior. See if they have anything to offer to your iPod playlist.

Develop a love of classical music. This guy has a definite love for the classics and will probably have no reservations about talking to you about them. Be it Beethoven or Mozart or Chopin, he'll provide insight into the lives and music of guys you simply knew as the original tortured geniuses.

245
If you're next to a composer ...

Debate barbecue. Memphis, Kansas City, Texas, and Lexington, North Carolina all claim to be the barbecue capital of the world. Folks who live in or near those places tend to be rabidly territorial about which barbecue is "real" barbecue. See what his opinion is on where the best BBQ comes from.

246
If you're next to a rib-eater ...

Find out where the best roller coaster is located. Any good thrill seeker has a favorite roller coaster. Whether it's because of its speed, or loops, or vertical thrust, see what she thinks is the most heart-pumping ride. Then plan a trip to the park and ride the coaster at your own risk.

247
If you're next to a thrill seeker ...

248

If you're next to a local ...

Ask about the regional shibboleths. Shibboleths are place names pronounced differently by different groups of people. For example, folks in the South know Biloxi, Mississippi, should be pronounced "buh-luck-see miss-sippy." People from Nevada know the "a" in the middle is like the "a" sound in "apple." When you ask for directions when you land, you will be prepared.

249

If you're next to a frugal local ...

Figure out the best deals in your destination city. Every city and town has hidden ways to save a buck. Whether it be farmers' markets, that concert in a town park on Thursdays, or bars that run happy hour specials, you can be certain there's a way to get by on a slimmer dollar wherever you travel. And the best way to do that is to ask a local. If you happen to be seated next to one, butter her up and ask her to divulge her spend-thrifty secrets.

250

If you're next to a travel agent ...

Rate hotels. Even though you're only in your room for a few hours each day, it can make a big difference as to how your experience goes. If you don't get the proper rest you need, your day of sightseeing will likely be cut short by exhaustion. You also don't want to be paying too much for a room that isn't even worth it. So, ask a travel agent for some free advice as to which hotels deliver the best deal for your dollar.

Debate how to fix the educational system. The accomplishments of America's children lag behind those of other developed nations. The government tries to fix the problem, but the programs often have little impact. See what someone on the front line thinks. Become informed about how the programs actually affect the students and teachers, and use this information when you weigh your voting decisions regarding the educational system.

251
If you're next to a teacher ...

Ask her opinion on the Great American Novel. Everyone in the English literature field has their own feeling on the ultimate American masterpiece. Let her give you her two cents on what should be considered the best of the American canon. You could debate her choice or take her insight to your next cocktail party.

252
If you're next to a literature professor ...

Share a list of favorite books. Librarians are *the* book people of all book people, and their lists of personal favorites cut across all genres and time periods. A quick, off-the-cuff top-ten list could easily provide you with months of entertaining reading.

253
If you're next to a librarian ...

254
If you're next to a publishing professional ...

Find out how to get published. Everyone thinks they have a book inside of them—even you. Take your random coupling as a sign that you're supposed to write your story and share it with the world. Ask him what he thinks the key points of a proposal are, what's the best method of submission, and if a literary agent is worth the cost. Don't forget to ask for his card so you can start calling him once your manuscript is finished.

255
If you're next to a meteorologist ...

Talk about the weather. Now that you're above the clouds, engage in the world's oldest conversational topic—the weather—with someone who knows all about it—or at least acts like it on television. Find out if he thinks the upcoming season will be a bad one and see if maybe he knows the difference between "partly sunny" and "partly cloudy."

256
If you're next to a paleontologist ...

Go *Jurassic*. Ask her what she thought of the movie *Jurassic Park*, which brought dinosaurs to life. Accurate! Far-fetched? Follow up and find out how she thinks the dinosaurs met their end.

Conquer your fear of numbers. If you're like most people, you hate math. (Unless you're the mathematician someone else is sitting next to.) Have him re-explain the theories you never quite caught on to in your high school classes. Maybe being so high will give you an elevated sense of learning.

257
If you're next to a mathematician ...

Find out how to avoid getting a speeding ticket. The easy answer is not to speed. But buy the guy a couple drinks and he might spill how to talk your way out of having to pay a hefty fine. Police officers are people too, and they will often take pity if you're in an unfortunate circumstance. See if that's something this cop believes when he pulls someone over. If not, ask him what he does fall for.

258
If you're next to a police officer ...

Discuss your irrational fears. Look, you know that mice are not going to bite you. They're more afraid of you than you are of them. But that doesn't stop you from screaming like a little girl when one appears from underneath your cabinets. What does this fear *really* mean? Try and squeeze out a few free minutes of therapy. Stop once she starts putting you on the clock.

259
If you're next to a psychiatrist ...

260
If you're next to an angler ...

Catch some fishing insight. The best way to learn how to do something is from the pros. If you happen to be seated next to master fisher, you can't pass up the opportunity to ask some questions. Chances are he'll enjoy spinning some fishing yarns for you. But make sure what he's telling you is the real deal and not just some "big fish" story.

261
If you're next to a gardener ...

Ask for some tips. Cultivating the perfect garden is truly an art form that takes a lot of practice, patience, and knowledge. Cheat your way to a picture-perfect garden by asking for some help. Explain the layout of your yard and the average amount of sunlight your garden area gets. See if she has any suggestions for the perfect plants to grow in those conditions.

262
If you're next to a chef ...

Gather some new recipes. What better way to pass the time than to talk about food? Find out what this chef's specialty is and then pump him for some flavorful recipes. Be sure to follow up and ask if he has any additional preparation or cooking tips so your next dish can come out restaurant-perfect.

Get some ideas for your home. Usually these types of professionals charge a pretty penny for their services. See if you can gather some free advice on what to do with your remodeling. Draw the layout of your current home, give him the details about your color scheme, and see if he can work some magic while you fly.

263
If you're next to an interior decorator ...

Get the cheats. Any good gamer knows about all the special hidden features of all his favorite games. If you're a video game enthusiast who just doesn't have any skills, see if this guy will drop some knowledge on you. Be it actual cheat codes or just helpful tips on how to beat a level's boss, his help will make your gaming experience a lot better.

264
If you're next to a gamer ...

Map out your expenses. Chances are, you have some trouble living within your means. Everyone does. That's why these types of people are so gainfully employed. Learn what you can do to budget your paycheck, stretch your bank account, and cover all your monthly expenses while still factoring in some leisure expenses.

265
If you're next to a financial planner ...

266
If you're next to an investment professional ...

Get some advice on the market. What's looking good now? See if she'll give you an inside track on a hot new stock that's making its way up the market. Consider it volunteer work, as she's helping to bridge the gap between Wall Street and Main Street. Hopefully, you can parlay her advice into a big payday.

MILE-HIGH MAKEOVERS

Come off this plane a changed person. Use this opportunity soaring above the ground as if it's your own reality makeover show. This chapter provides you with a whole host of ideas on how to go up one way and come down another. Some are superficial alterations to be made to your outer layer, while others are meant to change you from the inside out. What better place to try out a newer, better you than on a plane full of strangers? See what your in-flight friends think of the change, and if they like it, continue this new you on terra firma.

267
Give yourself a manicure and destroy your hangnails.

It's not quite the same as a visit to a nail salon, but you can still pamper yourself a bit. Bring along whatever you need—clippers, a nail file, fancy polishes, top-quality hand lotion. Put some soothing music on your headphones. In no time, you'll forget all about your cramped, lengthy flight.

268
Get a second opinion.

Your best friends won't always be honest with you, but total strangers might. If you've considered a new look, try it out for your seatmates before you debut it for colleagues and buddies. For that matter, solicit suggestions from seatmates for possible appearance changes. Listen to what they have to say, and don't take offense at their suggestions. You asked, remember?

269
Give yourself an unusual hairstyle.

Three-ounce cans of aerosol hairspray are acceptable on flights, so take advantage of this fact. Take your hairspray and comb or brush to the lavatory and sculpt an outlandish hairdo that will amaze and delight fellow passengers as well as those waiting for you on the ground.

Before you get on the plane, stop by a pharmacy and pick up a box of hair dye. Go to the bathroom and massage the dye in and then return to your seat while it sets. Head back to the restroom when it's time to wash it out and try your best at rinsing in that little sink. This may get messy, so take care when you're walking with the dye on your hands and hair. You don't want to rub up against anyone and leave an Auburn Light #7 smudge on your seatmate.

270
Dye your hair.

You're on vacation! You don't need all that makeup on anymore. Pack some facial cleanser or makeup remover in your carry-on and remove that face paint. Make it the symbolic removal of your day-to-day responsibilities.

271
Remove your makeup.

If you've got to go straight from the plane to an important business meeting, you need to look your best. Fortunately, safety razors are still acceptable on planes. Make sure your carry-on contains your razor and a travel-size can of shaving cream, and go to town on that five o'clock shadow.

272
Shave your hairy face.

273
Pluck your eyebrows.

Unless you're Frida Kahlo, you shouldn't be sporting a unibrow. Stick a set of tweezers and a vanity mirror in your carry-on. Once you're cruising, start plucking. Make sure the shape of your brows stays natural and compliments your features. Be careful of turbulence—one stray pluck and you may be investing in some eyebrow pencils.

274
Curl your lashes.

Make your lashes the curliest they've ever been. Eyelash curlers are acceptable on planes, so bring them with you and get to work. You'll be mistaken for a movie star before your plane touches the ground.

275
Decide how you can pamper yourself.

You work hard, and you deserve a rest. Come up with ways you can reward yourself for all you do. Avoid activities that can be counterproductive—drinking to excess, eating four double cheeseburgers—and focus on healthy methods. Perhaps you could buy some top-of-the-line bath salts and pledge to take a thirty-minute bath. You could go to the video store and rent the dumbest comedies on the market. The possibilities are endless.

If you've got dry, cracking skin, use your flight to slather yourself with lotion. Three-ounce containers of lotion are acceptable on flights. Remember not to pick something with an overpowering scent, which could cause fellow passengers to go reaching for an airsickness bag even when no turbulence is present.

276
Keep moisturized.

Sometime during the mid-1990s, tattoos became the newest permanent fashion accessory. Many folks chose Chinese characters, while others opted for illustrations that resemble mandalas. If you never took the tattoo plunge, it's not too late ... and you don't have to stab yourself with needles in the process. Just get out a pen and draw whatever design you like wherever you like.

277
Draw tattoos on your arms.

Most of us have terrible posture. We slump. We don't stand up straight. Over time, bad posture doesn't just make you look like a schlub, it actually can cause you health problems. Don't get old and stooped before your time. Concentrate on sitting up straight. Eventually your good posture will become a good habit.

278
Concentrate on your posture.

279
Schedule a workout regimen.

One half of a healthy life is daily exercise. However, you, like most people, are probably busy during the week. Take this break from the hustle to plan out a doable regimen. Don't overload yourself, as that's the first step to quitting. Plan on waking up a little earlier two or three days a week to go on a brisk morning jog. Decide on a muscle-set rotation so you don't wear yourself out—Monday's arms, Tuesday's legs, Wednesday's core, and so on.

280
Start a diet.

The other half of a healthy life is a well-balanced diet. Use the time you have to not only plan your exercise schedule, but to also set in place a new diet. Come up with a list of healthy foods you like and another list of your special treats for when you stick to your diet and exercise, and budget your new food plan.

281
Opt for cranberry juice.

When the flight attendant comes around with the drink cart, ask for cranberry juice rather than a carbonated beverage. Cranberry juice has been linked with several health benefits. It protects you against urinary tract infections, which sometimes can occur during disruptions to your daily routine (such as, say, lengthy flights). It also helps with gum infections, and it may help prevent heart disease. Carry this choice over to your daily life.

You may be tempted to stay away from peanuts because they have a high fat content. But the fat in most nuts is monounsaturated fat, which actually can help lower cholesterol and prevent heart disease. In addition, the protein in most nuts can lower your blood pressure. There's a reason Mr. Peanut is still going strong after ninety years!

282
Actually eat those peanuts.

You can't see them, but germs are everywhere, just waiting for their chance to pounce on you. Thwart them by washing your hands after you've visited the bathroom or after you've inadvertently touched something wet and slimy underneath your seat.

283
Wash your hands.

Most people don't brush and floss their teeth enough. Keep your toothbrush and floss in your carry-on, and put them to good use. Look at it this way: this healthy activity gives you a chance to get out of your seat for a little while. And if you've left your oral-health articles at home, at least keep some mints handy. Remember, the air on that plane keeps recirculating. Do your part to keep it from becoming foul.

284
Keep your breath minty fresh.

285
Put an end to a habit.

The only way to stop a habit is to, well, stop it. If you're a nail biter, for instance, then force yourself to leave your fingers alone during the entire flight. If you crack your knuckles, be cognizant of every time you start to do it. Once you've made a true commitment to cutting out a bad habit, it's easier to stretch that commitment and stop the habit altogether.

286
Lose your accent.

If you have a strong regional accent, it could affect your ability to rise through the ranks of your company. During your flight, practice speaking without a noticeable accent. Practice it on seatmates, who will be able to tell you how well you're doing (or not doing).

287
Practice your elocution and diction.

How now, brown cow? The rain in Spain falls mainly on the plains. Ten tame tadpoles tucked tightly in a thin tall tin. Repeat each of these sentences a few times, slowing your speech, and clearly pronouncing each syllable and word. You'll go from Eliza Doolittle to Meredith Viera in no time.

Pick up a pocket dictionary before you board the plane. Then spend part of your trip learning new words. The best way to do this is to look up any words you don't know in the book that you're reading.

288
Increase your vocabulary.

A proper gentleman or lady will never use contractions when he or she is speaking. Use the time you have onboard to rework the way you use everyday words like *I'm*, *won't*, *can't*, *shouldn't*, and *aren't*. I am telling you that you will not make a good impression on society's upper echelon if you cannot stop using these word combinations, as they should not be part of your vocabulary since they are not very proper.

289
Lose your contractions.

As a self-help guru recommended, you should recognize your self-worth and tell yourself, "I'm good enough, I'm smart enough, and doggone it, people like me." Granted, this self-help guru is actually comedian Al Franken dressed as Stuart Smalley, but nonetheless, he has a point! Appreciate yourself for who you are. Come up with a positive affirmation that applies to your life, then go to the restroom and repeat it in the mirror—just not too loud.

290
Repeat positive affirmations.

291
Make some resolutions.

They're not just for New Year's Day anymore. If there are things about yourself you want to change, write them down. Then brainstorm ways to make those changes take place. Finally, write down specific steps you can take to keep yourself motivated. You won't find a new you without a good set of instructions.

ALL BY YOURSELF

There's plenty to do all by yourself ... right? Right! Within this chapter, you'll find all sorts of activities to keep yourself busy when you're alone. Granted, you might need a little companionship (an iPod, laptop, or the like) to complete some of these, but for all intents and purposes, you're just playing by yourself.

292
Try to tickle yourself.

Go ahead, try it. First, use your fingers. Then use a pen or pencil. Finally, try using a tissue. You'll probably be at this the whole flight, as it's supposedly impossible to tickle yourself. But maybe you can. Wouldn't *that* be something to put on a resume? The only human being with the ability to tickle himself.

293
Sleep.

I know, what a boring suggestion for an entertaining thing to do on a plane. But have you actually ever tried to make yourself go to sleep? It's hard. So grab that tiny airplane pillow, strap on the sleep mask, and see if you can snooze. Allow your subconscious mind to wander free from the plane and do some important things, like solve life's problems or turn into a Viking.

294
Live (in) your dream.

Lucid dreaming is when you are aware that you are in fact dreaming and can alter what's happening in your dream. Try out the Mnemonic Induction of Lucid Dreams technique to take an active role in your dreams. As you're falling asleep, repeat in your head "I will remember I'm dreaming" and believe it. Falling asleep with this intention allows for a greater chance of lucid dreams—enjoy!

If you're one of those people who's never had a nickname but always wanted one, take your flight time to pull a George and solve the problem. Just as the *Seinfeld* character tried to pick his own nickname (T-Bone), bestow one upon yourself. Once you've chosen a nickname, introduce yourself to fellow passengers and make it stick—something George "Coco" Costanza couldn't pull off.

295
Give yourself a nickname.

Sudoku has swept the nation. The standard game uses a nine-by-nine grid containing nine three-by-three boxes. The goal is to place each digit from 1 to 9 in every row and column without repeating a digit in the same row, column, or three-by-three box. You can pick up a book of puzzles at any bookstore, and most newspapers run a puzzle in every edition. Just try not to make a mess with all the eraser bits and pulled-out hair.

296
One, two, three, sudoku!

You can either bring a deck of cards with you or opt for the computer version if you have a laptop. This simple card game can get quite addictive, as a failure to build a sequential order of cards by suit only leaves you wanting another chance. If you decide to play it old-school and go with a deck of cards, an added challenge to the game will be fitting the entire deck on that little tray table.

297
Play solitaire.

298
Peg solitaire, anyone?

Improvise your own "board" on the back of a cocktail napkin. Draw three horizontal rows of seven boxes. Intersect those three rows with three vertical rows of seven (the nine squares in the center should overlap). Use another napkin to make thirty-two small spitballs and place them in all the squares except for the center one—these are your "pegs." Begin jumping one peg over the other, removing the ones you hop, and try to leave just one peg in the middle.

299
Get to twiddlin'.

Thumb twiddling is the ultimate exercise for the bored and lazy. Anyone can twiddle his or her thumbs, but you can become a master of the art during your flight. Make up some twiddling moves that will leave spectators breathless and begging for more. And attempt the ultimate test of thumb twiddlin' expertise: getting one thumb to go clockwise and the other to go counter-clockwise at the same time. Think it's easy? Give it a try.

300
Up, over, down, over, down.

Fifteen puzzles are those little plastic square puzzles you used to get in the goody bags at birthday parties. Each puzzle is a four-by-four grid that contains fifteen small squares and one open space. The goal is to move the squares vertically and horizontally until they align into a picture or a sequential series of numbers. It's like a two-dimensional Rubik's cube.

It rocked the nation in the '80s and has remained on the shelves of kids (and their parents) to this day. An easy way to burn two, three, or fifteen hours is by trying to figure out this three-dimensional, multi-colored puzzle. The goal is get all the faces of the cube to be the same color. Getting there is a trip in itself. Bon voyage and happy twisting.

301

Solve a
Rubik's Cube.

Sick of suffering through your airline carrier's latest movie choice? Pick up a portable DVD player before your next flight. The cost of these sanity-saving devices continues to drop, so you can purchase one for rather cheap. Or you could just pop the disc into your laptop. Whatever your method, turning your tray table into a drive-in will have you laughing and crying the hours away.

302

Watch a DVD.

Over the past two decades, Nintendo's 8-bit handheld device has evolved into a 32-bit portable gaming console—and the perfect companion for any solo flyer. Nowadays, you'll find plenty of updates to your favorite Nintendo classics like Mario and Donkey Kong, as well as an updated version of the Game Boy staple, Tetris.

303

Game on
with your
Game Boy.

304
What's missing from your iPod?

Pop in your ear buds and cycle through your library. Go to the song collections of your favorite artists and make sure you have all their singles, albums, rarities, and collaborations. As you're listening to various songs with the intention of figuring out what you're missing, you'll inevitably remember a few that you need to download. Write them down and hit up the iTunes store when you land.

305
Name that iTune.

Some of the newer versions of the iPod have this fun game built in, but if you're still using an older model, it's no big deal, you can make it work on your own. Switch your player onto shuffle mode and allow a song to play for just three seconds. After three seconds, press the pause button and see if you can name that tune. Take a guess and check the display to see if you're right. Have a peanut or a shot for every one you get right.

306
Try some cryptograms.

Cryptograms are puzzles in which every letter in a phrase stands for another letter. The substitution remains consistent. For example, if S stands for I in the puzzle, you would replace every S with an I. These brainteasers can usually be found in any major newspaper. Ask the flight attendant if there are any newspapers to spare, flip to the puzzle's page, and start solving.

Before your trip, pick up a small puzzle, one with fewer than 500 pieces. Otherwise, it won't fit on your tray table. Once you're at cruising altitude, challenge yourself to complete the puzzle before you have to put your tray table back into its upright position.

307
Complete a jigsaw puzzle.

A kangaroo word is one that contains a smaller word that has the same, or nearly the same meaning as its "mother" word. For example, the word *rotund* contains the word *round*. Another stipulation to the kangaroo word rule is that the letters in the joey word, or synonym, must appear in consecutive order. So while *fiction* is a joey to *fabrication*, *craft* is not because the letters are scrambled. Skim through your reading material and look for them.

308
Find some kangaroo words.

If you're one of those annoying people who can't stand to see an apostrophe out of place, then you can use your time in the sky to find and correct mistakes in all available in-flight publications (even this book; I swear it won't hurt my feelings).

309
Whip out the red pencil.

310
Sharpen your memory.

A good memory is a key tool for success. The best way to keep it sharp is through constant practice. So take this time alone to give your memory a workout. Write down a series of seven numbers, review the numbers, then flip the piece of paper over and wait a minute. See if you can write down the same series of numbers from memory. Once you're able to recall seven numbers, move on to a series of ten, then twelve, and so on.

311
Ça va?

That's French for "What's up?" Now that your memory's sharp, see if you can remember "What's up?" in a variety of languages: *Ça va?* (French); *Qué pasa?* (Spanish); *Keefak?* (Arabic); *Wie getz?* (German); *Che?* (Italian). Now that you've memorized these quick phrases, you're on your way to being an international pickup artist.

312
Learn some card tricks.

Before your flight, pick up a deck of cards and a book of magic tricks. Spend your flight practicing the tricks. Once you've mastered a few, turn to your seatmate and try them out. He'll be amazed, and you'll feel like Houdini himself.

If you have a laptop with a Windows operating system, you most likely have Minesweeper. This addictive computer game has come installed with Windows since back when Windows 3.1 was released. The object is to use numbered clues to flag mines. Think you have what it takes to be a Minesweeper master? You better practice—the record completion of an expert level is thirty-seven seconds, and the intermediate level record is set at ten seconds!

313
Sweep for some mines.

Pi is the ratio of a circle's circumference divided by its diameter. Usually, you'll see it as 3.14, but the equation can be taken out to an infinite number of places. See how far you can take it. Use a circle with a circumference of 4 inches and a diameter of 1.27 inches to take pi out as far as you can (without falling asleep). It'll sharpen your math skills and give you something to talk about the next time you want an exit from an awkward conversation.

314
Look a pi in the face.

Admit it, you like doing word searches. It's okay, a lot of people do. The less intellectual sibling of the crossword doesn't get a lot of respect, but it's a fun way to pass the time. You might have more trouble finding a word search than a crossword, as they aren't usually run in newspapers—those elitists. So, pick up a cheap collection at your local bookstore or pharmacy and search away in the privacy of the plane.

315
Do a word search.

LISTS

It's time to really think—*really* think. A great way to pass the time while you're passing over land and water is to think about everything. And make a list. Some of these list prompts ask for the top ten (think: *Letterman*) of something and others ask for everything (think: *everything*) of everything. Take care with each entry. If you're making a top-ten list, be sure each entry really deserves to be on there. And if you're listing everything, take a moment to reflect on each listing as it's a part of your life, for better or for worse.

316

List every book you've ever read.

Whether you believe it or not, you've read a lot of books in your lifetime. On top of everything you read for school, think back to children's books you read in your youth, the young adult novels you pored over, and all the popular fiction that kept you turning pages. Take a minute to remember each book and reflect on how its story affected your life. Keep this list handy, as you'll surely be adding to it as another book conquered comes to mind.

317

List every movie you've ever seen.

If the books list was difficult, this one is going to be a mission. You not only need to write down the favorites you spent months in anticipation for, but also those matinees watched from the comfort of your couch on rainy Saturdays. Remember the experience each brought as you list it, the date you went on, the friends you went with, the thrill you felt the first time you saw it.

318

List every city you've ever visited.

Don't just write down the big ones—New York City, London, Rio, Rome, Los Angeles, Sydney—be sure you include all the little ones you stopped in and visited, be it the daylong layover in Raleigh, or the night you spent in Topeka during a cross-country trip. Each of these cities is a different memory; think about where you've been on your way to somewhere else.

It's okay to kiss and tell if it's just for a private list. I won't tell anyone. Be it on a recent date or way back when, during a game of spin the bottle, make sure you cover every one of the people you've swapped spit with.

319
List every person you've ever made out with.

Take the above prompt a step further and circle all those people with whom you've rounded home. Don't worry, there's no magic number for this list. You may think your list has too few entries, and the person next to you may believe theirs has five too many. It doesn't matter about the number, just the moment. Relive each moment now that you have some time alone.

320
List every person you've ever slept with.

You should really take time with this list in particular. Which of these people are you no longer in contact with? How do you feel about that? Is it something you can remedy? Making good friends is hard, keeping them is work, but losing them only takes one bad decision. See how your list shapes up and figure out what you can and cannot rectify.

321
List every friend you've ever made.

322
List your favorite childhood television shows.

Every generation feels that its kids' shows were the best and that the current crop pales in comparison. What were your favorites? Start your list by thinking of all the ones you can remember and then go through and select your favorites. Choose wisely.

323
List every regret you've ever had.

Some people may have a very short list—if any list at all. Those are the "live with no regrets" kind of people. Good for them (and for you if you're one of them). But more than likely, you've made a few bad decisions. Admit it. Writing them down will be the first step in feeling better and getting over them.

324
List the top ten happiest moments of your life.

Really think about this one. What events have truly made you happy? It may be a monumental instance, like your wedding or the birth of your child. Or it may be something that seems trivial but that resonates with you to this day, like the first time you went fishing with your father. Reflect on each moment you choose and relive it as you soar through the sky.

The worst times in your life have just as much importance in shaping who you are as the happiest times. What are the ten misfortunes that had an impact on the person you have become? These may end up being harder to decide on than the happiest moments in your life.

325
List the top ten saddest moments of your life.

It may seem like a tedious process, but these people have all had an impact on your professional life. What lessons have you learned from each one? Some people are meant to be role models in your life and others are meant to be examples on how *not* to live your life. Think about how each of these people has shaped who you are in your career as you list their names.

326
List every coworker you've ever worked with.

These cultural institutions provide a personal experience. Be it an art museum, history museum, or science museum, every one of them has helped you learn at least one concept or piece of knowledge you carry with you to this day. As you generate this list, remember the lesson you took from each entry.

327
List every museum you've ever visited.

328
List every teacher you've ever had.

The easiest way to do this is to go grade by grade and write down the teacher who led your classroom that particular year. Then go back through time and recognize those people who helped teach you outside of the classroom: parents, coaches, family, friends.

329
List the top ten scariest moments of your life.

Any near-death experiences in your past? If so, it's probably a gimme for the list. Otherwise, you'll have to think about those moments in your life where you thought you were going to lose someone or something important to you. Coming up with this list will help you realize who and what is truly important in your life.

330
List the top ten lies you've ever told.

Unless you're Honest Abe, you've definitely told a lie. And it's a likely bet that at least a couple have been real doozies. As you narrow down your list, make sure all the entries have been resolved. If you realize something hasn't and that lie is still present in your life, rectify the situation with the person you lied to once you get off the plane. Life's too short to be spent wrapped up in lies.

Granted, the saying goes: It's better to give than to receive. But take this time alone to think about the ones you've been given. They don't have to be extravagant. They just have to still ring true as something you really enjoyed receiving. You might even drop a belated thank-you card or two in the mail once you decide on your final ten.

331
List the top ten gifts you've ever received.

You'll need to ask the flight attendant for some extra napkins to complete this one, as it's undoubtedly going to be one of the longest. Each time you add one to your list, try to remember the first time you heard it. Where were you? What were you doing? Who were you with?

332
List every song you've ever heard.

Vacations are the harbors of our sanity. You might even be going on one now, which will—fingers crossed—make its way onto this list. Don't count out the short weekend trips you took with your family to local destinations. Sometimes the simplest vacation can be the best.

333
List the top ten vacations you've ever taken.

334

List the ten worst dates you've ever been on.

Now that you've had some time to recover from the emotional scarring of these awful instances, take a minute to laugh about them. Whether the negative experience was your fault or the fault of your date or the person who set you up, realize that it's over. And it's time to enjoy it now that you're at a safe distance.

335

List every restaurant you've ever eaten in.

It might sound trivial, but even these places have had some influence on who you have become. That is because a restaurant is not only a place to eat, but also a place to gather and enjoy the company of friends and family. Think of the ones where special events happened, the old regulars you went to with your family, and favorite hangouts you'd go to with your friends whenever you got together.

FOR THE LAYOVER

The layover. It's been known to ruin many an air adventure with its hours upon hours of dead time. There are only so many trips you can take around the terminal before you want to jump in front of an oncoming baggage cart. These ideas on what to do when you're stuck sitting in Des Moines International will help keep the edge off the mind-atrophying layover.

336
Get landscaping ideas.

Believe it or not, airports often have some of the prettiest landscaping you will see. Perhaps the airport's board of directors knows that the airport may be the one place you will see in Atlanta, St. Louis, or Phoenix, so the area's best face is put forward. As you walk around the airport during your layover, check out its use of native shrubs, plants, and flowers. Feel free to steal ideas for your own use back home.

337
Look at the public art.

Most airports have more than grossly overpriced food and drinks. They actually have commissioned local and regional artists to create work that is displayed throughout the terminal. The work often reflects the area's culture, and some of it is quite beautiful. You might lose some of your stress if you imagine yourself walking through a very large, very crowded public art gallery rather than through a very large, very crowded airport.

338
Find the historical displays.

As mentioned, many airports have public art, but some also have displays related to local history. Sometimes these displays are fascinating and will help you to learn information about the area's part in aviation history, the Civil War, manufacturing, or Native American history. If you have to be stuck in the airport, at least you can make it an educational inconvenience.

Admit it. It's fun. Try crouching down slowly so that, to others, you'll appear to be sinking as you ride along. Or try holding yourself up off the track by balancing on the moving arm rails. Ride it backward. Use your imagination and have fun with it. Who cares what others think? You'll never see those people again!

339
Ride that moving sidewalk again and again.

Walking around is way overrated—especially when those speedy little golf carts are whizzing around everywhere. Why should the aged and infirm have all the fun? Use your powers of persuasion to hitch rides on the cart. Compete with your friends to see who can con the most rides.

340
Hitchhike in the terminal.

Your town might fit in one of those colossal airports such as Atlanta's Hartsfield-Jackson. Atlanta's airport has subways, miles of tunnels, a shopping mall, fine restaurants, and practically every other creature comfort imaginable. If you're on a long layover, take some time to explore the four corners of the airport. Just don't get lost. You wouldn't want to miss your connection.

341
Explore the four corners.

342
Try to find a comfortable nap spot.

Take a leisurely stroll around your terminal and look for the best napping spot. See if there are any rows of chairs without armrests, or search for a spot on the floor behind a potted plant, where it's unlikely you'll be trampled. Just remember to set your cell phone's alarm so you don't miss your flight!

343
Decorate your luggage.

Nowadays, your carry-on has to be like an extra appendage once you're inside the airport, so take some time to decorate it. As you're dutifully not leaving your bag unattended, break out some markers or patches or cloth and turn your duffle bag into a one-of-a-kind.

344
Hunt for the ugliest tie.

The uniform for most male business travelers is the business suit. Some are even made to stay wrinkle-free even when wadded in a suitcase. And to be complete, it requires a tie. Ties can be powerful and bold. They can be jaunty and amusing. And they can be just plain butt-ugly. Kill some time and look for the hands-down, no-contest ugliest tie. Just make sure it's not your own!

Most airports have a visitors' center that contains local information. Once you find the visitors' center, pick up all the brochures for area attractions. It will kill time, and you may find someplace you'll want to visit during another trip. If you don't finish reading all the brochures by departure time, you can always take them with you on the plane.

345

Read through area brochures.

The visitors' center in most airports contains racks of real estate publications. You can fantasize about changing your life by moving to a new place and getting a new start. You can compare the cost of living in your hometown to that of your layover city. You might even get ideas for ways to improve your own home's curb appeal.

346

Check out local real estate.

As you patiently sit in your seat waiting to board your delayed connection, take a minute to drift off and daydream. Leave the hustle and bustle of the busy airport and let your mind wander. It's usually best if you can do this near a window with a view that isn't obstructed by a radio tower or commercial airliner.

347

Daydream.

348
Watch planes take off and land.

It doesn't matter that flight is a common occurrence. There's still something exciting and awe-inspiring about watching large, ungainly steel objects launch into the air and return to land. Plus, you'll be less jittery after you've watched countless planes take off and land safely and without incident.

349
Count the number of airlines.

The number of airlines an airport carries is proportionate to the health of the city's business community. If there are few airlines or some check-in counters that have been abandoned, the town's economic future may not be rosy. If, on the other hand, the airport has several airlines—including ones unfamiliar to you—then it's probably a city that's on the way up.

350
Play airline bingo.

If you've made a buddy during the first half of your flight, you can set up a friendly layover game of "spot that plane." Grab a couple of seals next to a window where you can see several different planes taxiing around the runway. See how many different airline logos you can spot. Call out the airline, show your competitor where the plane is, and claim your point.

Visit the airport's visitors' center and speak with the very knowledgeable folks who staff it. Kill some time talking to the tourist information agents. You'll find out all sorts of information about local history and hideaways, including the ones typical tourists don't usually visit. See what kind of attractions your stopover city has to offer—maybe you'll even want to extend your layover on the way back.

351
Talk to tourist information agents.

Airports often have a "rental-car row" filled with the stalls of different rental companies. If you have time to kill, go to each and compare rates for the same type of car. Even if you don't need a rental car during this trip, you will get an idea of which companies offer the best deals, should you need a rental car in the future.

352
Compare rental rates.

Soon, you'll be sitting again for a long, long time. Take advantage of your delayed connection by strapping your carry-on to your back and hitting whatever stairs you can find—over and over and over again. You'll get a great leg workout and you'll also tire yourself so it'll be easier to sleep once you get on the plane.

353
Get some exercise.

354
Do some jumping jacks.

Man, you've just been sitting down for hours! As soon as you get from tarmac to terminal, drop your carry-on and start some calisthenics. All that blood that's settled in your hindquarters will return to your brain, where it belongs.

355
Practice yoga.

Find yourself a nice open spot in your connecting terminal and stretch into some yoga positions. Work out all the kinks that the first leg of your trip built up with a downward facing dog. Don't mind all the stares you're getting. Those people are just jealous because they can't twist and bend like you.

356
Listen to other people's conversations.

Be a spy. Circulate around the waiting area and listen covertly to other people's discussions and arguments. Most likely, you'll find that your life isn't so bad compared to the trials and tribulations others endure. You may even get fodder for a story you could write on the plane.

Raw human emotion is a scintillating sight, and it's in full bloom when families separate at the airport. Stand on the sidelines and watch as moms, dads, wives, husbands, kids, friends, and lovers say tearful, emotional goodbyes to one another. It's sure to renew your faith in humankind.

357
Watch others' goodbyes.

Even if you've outgrown them, video games are a great way to pass time while sharpening your hand-eye coordination. Most airports have a sizable game room. Find it, and spend all the quarters you've brought with you. Go for that high score, and proudly add your initials to the screen.

358
Play video games.

Airports have tons of drink and snack machines. And they have legions of people in a hurry. Put the two together, and you're likely to find a treasure trove of spare change underneath the vending machines. Ignore your dignity, and go on a hunt for hidden treasure.

359
Hunt for change.

360
Get a shoeshine.

Most airports, even small ones, have little shoeshine stands. These throwbacks to a simpler time often are manned by folks who have been in the airport since Orville and Wilbur Wright were pups. Get a shine. Listen to the shoeshine operator's stories. And don't forget to leave a large tip when you're done.

361
Buy stamps and send mail.

Most airports have a self-service post office center at which you can buy books of stamps and prestamped postcards. You'll also find a mailbox. If you've got bills to pay, bring them with you to the airport to kill time while you wait for your flight. You can buy the postage for your bills and correspondence and mail the letters and bills prior to your flight.

362
Call someone.

You're alive! You made it—halfway! Give your loved ones an update as to where you are in your journey. Tell them all about fellow passengers' peccadilloes and share the plot of the in-flight movie. If they're picking you up at your destination, be sure to update them on whether or not one or more of your flights have been delayed, or if you're possibly ahead of schedule. Oh, and don't forget to say "I love you."

Sit in the terminal where your connection is coming into and count the number of people in the same circumstance as you. This is a two-fold relaxation method. For one, the counting will put your nerves at ease, and for two, realizing all these people are in the same situation as you will make you feel better about waiting.

363
Count the number of people waiting.

You can find melatonin supplements in most airport drugstores. Some people swear that these little homeopathic pills are a magical cure for jet lag. If you have about a half-hour before you get back onboard, track down and take a dose of the supplements. They can help you sleep during the flight. That way, you're more likely to avoid that dreaded jet lag.

364
Take your melatonin.

If you're with your family, make a friendly wager as to when your connecting flight will actually roll up to the terminal. Even if the plane is on time, it likely will be just a little early or a wee smidge late. See who's closest to the actual arrival time. The losers have to do the winner's chores for a day when you get home.

365
Take bets on your flight's arrival time.

366
Trade delay horror stories.

Once you're in the air, you can get anywhere in a reasonable time. But a delayed flight due to severe weather can leave you stranded for hours, perhaps even days. Fortunate travelers are stuck in the terminal. Unfortunate ones can be stranded on their planes. If you've got a delayed-flight "horror story," share it with other folks awaiting their flights. Most likely, they've got a story or two themselves.

367
Keep up with current events.

If you're a businessperson on the go, you may not always have time to read the newspaper—online or otherwise. You may go several days between visits to your favorite media blog. Don't be dismayed! Almost all airports show continuous news channels such as CNN Headline News on screens all over the terminal. In no time, you can be up on the latest world and national events, as well as on all the celebrity gossip and scandal.

368
Give to charity.

Just because you can't give millions to end hunger or AIDS doesn't mean you shouldn't give anything. Most charitable organizations depend on small donations, which come from folks just like you. Airports usually offer one if not a few different charitable opportunities. Get out that checkbook and hunt down a worthy cause, whether it's a UNICEF stand or the collection box for the Ronald McDonald House at the counter of the airport's Mickey Ds.

If you've recently gotten engaged, or have a birthday coming up, or it's around the holidays, go through the various stores and make a list of everything you want. This way you have a response when someone asks, "Well, what do you want?"

369
Make a list of potential gifts.

Cherish the time you spent in ... wait, where are you again? The layover city is an important part of your journey. So celebrate your time there with some sort of novelty purchase. Come on, admit it—you always wanted a coffee cup labeled "Topeka."

370
Buy some layover city swag.

A requisite shop at most airports is the bookstore. This is where travel-weary passengers pick up their journey's distractions; be it books or magazines. Flip ahead to Suggested Reading on page 207 to get some ideas on what you should pick up.

371
Browse the bookstore.

372
Have a drink.

Now that you're off that flying torture chamber, have a double to calm your nerves. Drinking during the flight itself doesn't really make you feel any better, and it could wind up making you do something stupid enough to cause an international incident.

373
Avoid coffee.

If you want to avoid jet lag, stay away from coffee. It may give you a temporary lift, but it dehydrates you. Experts aren't sure if caffeine actually causes jet lag, but they agree that caffeine makes jet lag's symptoms worse. Keeping yourself hydrated will help you to adjust better to a new time zone.

374
Get some real food.

Even if the only places available are fast-food joints, go immediately to one and have some real, nonairline food. Stuff your face with burgers. Slather your fries with a gallon of ketchup. Get refill after refill from the drink machine. Then find the nearest doughnut shop and engulf even more fat grams.

You've been wearing the same outfit since Newark. Chances are you're feeling pretty gross and might even be putting off somewhat of a funk. Pull out that extra set of clothes and go to the bathroom to freshen up. Your new seatmate will thank you.

375
Change your clothes.

Finally, you're able to sit in front of those big airport windows and soak in the sun. Let it beat down on your face. Realize—perhaps for the first time—how truly wonderful it is to have the sun shine down on you. Unless of course, it's nighttime.

376
Enjoy the sun!

GET CREATIVE

When was the last time you had a few minutes to just be creative? Fifth-grade art class? Thought so. Seize the day! Take advantage of the time you have and the things around you. Have yourself a little arts and crafts session to remind you of those hours at summer camp spent weaving bracelets, or rainy childhood afternoons reserved for imaginative conversations. Since you're stuck sitting in an upright position, you might as well let the creative juices flow and get a sweet new potholder out of the whole ordeal.

377

Create a new identity.

"Schwartz. Chuck Schwartz." It just doesn't have the ring of "Bond. James Bond," does it? So re-create yourself. You're not about to give a business presentation in Dubuque. You're a secret agent. Or a character actor. Or a famous, reclusive author. The possibilities are endless. By the time you deplane, your seatmates will be clamoring for your autograph.

378

Fold, fold, crease, fold, *voilà*!

Origami, the Chinese art of creative paper folding, has existed for thousands of years. You can twist simple pieces of paper into frogs, cranes, or any number of other objects. Visit *www.origami-usa .org* before your next flight and print out some patterns. All you need to bring with you is paper, or you could use some currency. Think of the reactions you'll get when you pay for that hot dog with a swan-shaped five-dollar bill!

379

Weave bracelets.

Any craft store will have the materials with which to weave bracelets. It's a time-consuming creative activity that could even result in some profit. After you've woven several during your flight, you can hand them out as gifts to your friends.

Pick up some rubber stamps and an ink pad at your local craft store. Put several plain white envelopes in your carry-on bag. During your flight, use the rubber stamps to make custom envelopes. You can use the envelopes for the birthday and/or holiday cards you send to friends and family.

380
Make custom envelopes.

Does it have a harvest gold kitchen and six-inch deep shag rugs? Is the indoor swimming pool in the foyer between the front door and the living room? Does it have hardwood floors and a knotty pine bar with antlers adorning the wall above your built-in bar? Whether it's a McMansion or a modest bungalow, spend your air time designing the perfect home.

381
Design your dream house.

The Byrds are credited with creating "country rock" on their album *Sweetheart of the Rodeo*. Stephen Wiley was the first artist to release an album of Christian rap, 1985's *Bible Break*. Miles Davis was a pioneer of jazz fusion. His album, *Bitches Brew*, fused jazz and rock sensibilities. Surely there's some sort of music fusion yet to be created. What could you combine? If you can marry two divergent types of music, you might well make a fortune.

382
Create a new music fusion.

383
Design a squirrelproof birdfeeder.

How do those cute, fluffy rodents do it? They must have magical powers of levitation! It doesn't seem to matter where you hang your birdfeeder; the squirrels muscle away the songbirds you're trying to attract. Some companies have manufactured so-called "squirrelproof" birdfeeders, but there's always room for new ideas. See if you can devise something that truly will keep the squirrels at bay. If you can, you'll make a million dollars in no time flat.

384
Come up with a piece of modern conceptual art.

Marcel Duchamp took a urinal and displayed it as a work of art named "Fountain." That piece, which he called a "readymade," is one of the most influential pieces in modern art history. Contemporary conceptual art makes the familiar strange and the common uncommon. Put your mind to modern art. Picture an art museum, a huge space with white walls. What could you put in there that could turn the art world on its collective ear?

385
Make a mobile.

Prior to your flight, go by a craft store and pick up some yarn and pipe cleaners. Bring them, along with safety scissors, onto the plane. Spend your flight cutting out interesting photos from the SkyMall catalog and in-flight magazine. Then use the yarn and pipe cleaners to fashion the photos into a mobile you can hang in your cubicle.

Political cartoons seek to satirize the political landscape. Often caricatures of well-known personalities are married to symbolic objects used to reflect current issues. A cartoon might feature an ocean liner run aground. The captain is the president, and the liner is labeled "ship of the state." The message is that the president has screwed up. Try your hand at drawing political cartoons. Politicians and famous people are always doing stupid things.

386
Draw a political cartoon.

You spent the previous night at a motel and you pilfered one of those tiny soaps from your bathroom. That little cake of soap is still with you. Now you're finishing up your in-flight meal, and you've got a plastic knife just sitting there. Put the knife to good use. Use it to carve the soap into simple shapes, such as a heart or a diamond.

387
Try soap carving.

Chunky Monkey. Cherry Garcia. Phish Food. Not only are Ben & Jerry's ice creams great, they have some of the greatest names in marketing. Even though the company has gone corporate, you can still help out Ben & Jerry. Come up with a list of new flavor names and the flavors that each would incorporate. Send the list in to them. Who knows? Your flavor may wind up in your grocer's freezer section.

388
Make up new Ben & Jerry's flavors.

389
Design the World's Weirdest Building.

Some might say the Mitchell, Kansas, Corn Palace already owns this title, but why not come up with an even weirder design than a minareted building covered with corn murals? Come up with a skyscraper that looks like Bob the Builder or a civic building that looks like a sleeping giant. The possibilities are endless!

390
Cross-stitch.

Cross-stitching is similar to paint-by-numbers kits. You take a pattern, available at craft stores, and stitch different-colored threads through the pattern to create designs. You might cross-stitch a decorative pillow for a new grandchild, for example. Airplane-acceptable synthetic needles can be used for your project.

391
Invent a new reality show.

Reality shows began to take over the airwaves in the late 1990s. Networks love them because they're cheap to produce. They don't feature A-list stars with A-list salaries, after all. Audiences love them because these shows appear to "keep it real" and offer moments of genuine drama: Who will be voted off the island? Who will be fired? Who will the star start a catfight with next? Use your flight time to come up with a new reality show concept.

Some folks believe that our universe is only one of many that coexist in the same place at the same time. These mysterious parallel universes are sometimes blamed for so-called supernatural events. Create your own parallel universe. What do the people there look like? What do they do all day? What laws of time and space does this universe follow?

392
Build a parallel universe.

If you have several old pieces of material moldering away in your closet, cut them up into small pieces, bring them with you on the plane, and take on a patchwork project. Patchwork is the process of taking those scraps, or patches, and stitching them together to form new, larger items, such as quilts. Synthetic needles, acceptable on planes, can be used for your project.

393
Try some patchwork.

Crochet is the art of creating decorative fabric from yarn, wire, or thread. All that's needed is the yarn and a crochet hook, which can be picked up at any craft store (they're allowed on planes). Basically, you use the hook to create a chain of fabric. Projects for beginners also are available at any craft shop.

394
Crochet.

395
Make some jewelry.

Even small towns have bead shops, which sell all manner of tiny, colorful glass and plastic baubles. Pick up some of these and use them to fashion necklaces, bracelets, and other jewelry you can give as personalized gifts to friends and business clients.

396
Start a scrapbook.

A scrapbook is just that—a collection of scraps that reflect your life. Look around you. What could you take from this particular flight to put in a book? For starters, there's your boarding pass. You could rip a page from the in-flight magazine. Keep the napkin you're given. Hey—it's your life! It's worth preserving.

397
Knit a sweater.

Knitting needles are acceptable on planes. Knitting is a time-consuming, meticulous craft, so it's perfect for a lengthy flight. Beginners' books and projects are available at craft stores and at many department stores as well.

Calligraphy is the art of using a fountain pen to create lettering that looks like art. Calligraphy requires patience and discipline, and it is still a staple on such items as invitations. You can pick up an instructional book at the local bookstore or library and a fountain pen and "fancy" paper at most greeting card stores. Just watch out for turbulence!

398
Practice calligraphy.

Ron Popeil has marketed some of humankind's greatest inventions: the Miracle Broom, the food dehydrator, the Veg-O-Matic, and everyone's favorite: Mr. Microphone. Popeil, founder of Ronco, transformed these and other odd objects into things you simply could not live without. He's still going strong. See if you can come up with some new inventions for Popeil to hawk on cable channels during the predawn hours.

399
Come up with new Ronco inventions.

Vanity license plates give you the chance to put your personal stamp on your car. Come up with your own plate. Remember, it will need to be no more than seven letters and/or numbers long—and please pick something that others might understand. Who knows how many accidents have occurred while someone is trying to figure out an indecipherable vanity plate in front of him?

400
Come up with your own vanity plate.

401
Collaborate and perform.

Are you a creative, outgoing person? Are you fortunate enough to be seated near like-minded individuals? Great! Work with your seatmates and write a play for the three or four (or however many) of you. Each person should focus on the actions of his or her character. Then try performing the play. Somewhere in the midst of the production, switch roles.

402
Start your own secret society.

Secret societies don't want you to know what goes on during their meetings. They often give the sense that something sinister is going on behind those closed doors. Secret societies include Yale University's Skull and Bones, the Mafia, and the Illuminati. Come up with your own tricked-out society name; decide who you would like to recruit for members; set a strict code of conduct and testing process for your perspective members.

403
Start your family tree.

Begin a family tree by placing on it all the relatives you can remember, even if they're twice removed. You'll probably find that you remember a sizable number of blood relations. Once you've begun your tree, you can continue your genealogical research when you return home.

Duct tape is one of the world's modern wonders. It seems capable of fixing anything. A roll of it is even included on space shuttle missions! Back on the ground, people use duct tape to make wallets and bandages, and to tape drunken friends to the chairs in which they've passed out. How many more uses can you come up with for this wonder substance?

404
Come up with uses for duct tape.

Who can forget "Life's a beach, then you die" or "Sh*t happens"? These immortal, pithy words of wisdom sold oodles of T-shirts and made someone somewhere pretty wealthy. Come up with your own piece of T-shirt literature. Test it out on other passengers. If your new slogan gets a thumbs-up, hit up a Web site like *www.cafepress.com* when you land and start printing your tees.

405
Come up with a new T-shirt slogan.

ROMANCE AT 30,000 FEET

Want a way to *really* make the flight entertaining? Use your cabin as your own personal Match.com. Pick out a potential mate who's traveling alone (or not alone, if you're up for a challenge). Use your manly or womanly wiles and work your magic with these great ideas to get steamy at 30,000 feet.

406
Hey baby, what's your sign?

Asking someone for her zodiac sign invokes the cheesiest come-on lines of the 1970s—the world's cheesiest decade. Use that to your advantage; accept the fact that you're being cheesy and work it to your advantage. This self-awareness will come off as confidence, and confidence is always a good thing.

407
Read her palm.

You mean you don't know how to translate the creases and folds of her palm into an actual fortune? Oh well. Simply getting her to place her palm in your hand is enough of an advance. As long as you hold her hand with a delicate strength and look into her eyes, it really won't matter what you're saying.

408
Give her a massage.

Again, it's all about the touching. This doesn't need to be a full-on back massage or even a neck rub. You can begin your intimacy by gently massaging her hand. Use your thumb to work her palm and move your fingers around on the back of her hand. If she suggests the massage move on to other locations, follow her lead!

A great icebreaker to lighten the mood and ease any sexual tension is to joke about everyone else around you. It keeps the conversation off the two of you, while building a bond between you and him. You're making up these names for your own secret entertainment. Pretty soon you'll both be comfortable with one another and can move on to other things.

409
Come up with nicknames for everyone around you.

You can't join the Mile-High Club with a stranger until he is no longer a stranger. He's most likely way more into it than you are, so playing hard to get may work to you advantage. Toy with him a little and it will leave him only wanting more.

410
Seduce him.

Show off your bartending skills as you order up some of those tiny liquor bottles from the flight attendant. Stir in a couple pours from one of those half-sized soda or juice cans and you'll have yourself a tasty cocktail. Your liquor options are going to be slim, so stick with some basic drinks like a Cape Codder (vodka and cranberry juice), a Seven and Seven (whisky and 7-Up), or an Opal (gin and orange juice—and Triple Sec if available).

411
Mix her a drink.

412
Share a glass of fine wine.

Set the mood up right. You can't bring a bottle from home, but if your airport has a duty-free shop, you should be able to buy fine wine there and take it onto your flight. Corkscrews also are available on planes, so once you're airborne, open the wine and share it with fellow passengers.

413
Who's the hottest?

Depending on how open your partner is, you could see if she's interested in scoping out the other ladies onboard. You can easily play this to your advantage. No matter who she picks out, tell her how they pale in comparison to her and how much hotter she is than her. Compliments will get you everywhere.

414
Envision the perfect hotel room.

As you sit there relaxing on your mile-high date, think about the ultimate romantic getaway. Imagine aloud about how you picture the perfect hotel room. What type of bed would it have? Where would it be located? What special little extras would it come complete with?

This may sound like the last thing you would want to do in order to make the mood more romantic. However, if you each take time venting, there's a better chance that you'll pick up on what pisses each other off, and therefore avoid such things. When your relationship is moving as fast as yours is—literally at jet speed—you need as much help and as many shortcuts as possible.

415
Vent to each other.

Remember this little game? It's a great way to test the inhibitions of the person you're flirting with. It's also a great way to help lose any inhibitions he may actually have. Take turns saying, "Never have I ever ..." and filling in the blank with some sort of sexual escapade. If the other person has done whatever you say, he would take a sip of his drink.

416
Never have I ever ...

You only have a little time to work your angle on the person you're flirting with, so pull out all the stops. Remember, you'll probably never see this person again—unless you *really* hit it off. Let her hear about the true you and, in return, listen to what makes her tick.

417
Bare your soul.

418
Watch a DVD.

Break out your portable DVD player or laptop and stick in a romantic movie. Don't go for anything too melodramatic, but make sure it plays up the sensual. You want something that will get both of you in the mood, without turning either one of you off. A few suggestions: *Unfaithful*, *9½ Weeks*, and *Eyes Wide Shut*.

419
Look at the constellations.

What's more romantic than looking up at the stars? Cruising through the sky as they dot the distance! There's no need to look up, and this helps your positioning. Have her lean on your shoulder to get a better view if you have the window seat. You can either keep talking or just stare into the distance.

420
Don't forget his phone number.

Before things get too carried away, make sure you grab his digits so you can meet up if you get split up at baggage claim. The two of you have made such a connection already, it'd be horrible if you forgot to exchange numbers.

It might sound like a topic to avoid, but it's one that might open up even more lines of communication between you and your new romantic interest. How does she feel about marriage? About divorce? About premarital sex?

421
Discuss marriage.

Start a list of pop culture's truest pairings. These fictional relationships have achieved the status you could only dream about for yours. This conversation may lead to more in-depth relationship talk, so reader beware.

422
Luke and Laura, Ross and Rachel, Zack and Kelly ...

Dropping this on the flight attendant may get you moved up to first class. Tell the flight attendant you're newlyweds and you're flying to your honeymoon destination. Even if you don't get the bump up to first class, you might some free champagne.

423
Say you just got married.

424
Propose marriage.

Why stop at just faking a marriage? Love is in the air! You're in the clouds, close to heaven, flying through the air on gossamer wings. Pop the ultimate question! Why not? You can always change your mind once you hit the tarmac.

425
Communicate without speaking.

A very sensual activity is to look directly in the eyes of whomever you're with and not say a word. Just allow your eyes to speak with that person's. Try not to break eye contact, not even to blink. Stare into her soul and let her peer into yours—the better she knows you, the luckier you may get.

426
Join the Mile High Club.

When two people love each other, they make the adult decision to consummate their feelings by engaging in lovemaking. When two people meet on a plane, have a few drinks, and feel adventurous, they make the spontaneous decision to consummate whatever they're feeling in an airliner's lavatory. Find a willing partner and leave the rest of the passengers wondering: Is that turbulence or just good, fine lovin'?

If this really, truly feels like the real thing, don't let it go. Make plans to meet up again if you're heading in separate directions once the plane lands. While it may be fun to keep this as a one-time impulsive tryst, maybe this was actually meant to be *it*. If the two of you end up getting married, though, you'll have to spend your honeymoon just flying around in planes.

427
Plan to meet up once you get off.

Okay, so things didn't pan out the way you intended, and there wasn't a fellow passenger whom you felt you clicked with. Move on to a flight attendant. Don't be too obvious or too forceful about it, but you never know, you may even get lucky ... or at least a dinner companion in Newark.

428
Hit on the flight attendant.

OFFICE ONBOARD

Sometimes it takes some time out of the office to really get on top of what's going on inside the office. With meetings and e-mails and phone calls and drop-ins, there are some days you feel as if you've accomplished nothing. Use your time up above to help your career. Whether you spend it doing the small office tasks you never get around to or really take a moment to look at where you are in your career, you can capitalize on having some time away from your desk to get ahead.

429
Do that pesky paperwork.

Admit it. You've got reams of paperwork shoved to a corner of your desk. You've tried to hide this disorganized blob with other papers, coffee cups, and pictures of your loved ones. But those papers are still there, haunting you every day. Bring them with you onto the plane, and complete those annoying, albeit necessary, little paperwork tasks that you can never find time to do.

430
Make presentation flash cards.

Even though you're likely to use Power-Point or similar software for your next business presentation, it never hurts to rely on an old standby from your school days: flash cards. Bring some index cards with you. On one side, write key terms or concepts. On the other, write sentences using those terms and concepts. Then use the cards to help you prepare even more thoroughly for your looming presentation.

431
Organize your BlackBerry.

When was the last time you went through and deleted all those old e-mails and phone messages? As long as you turn your BlackBerry's wireless off, you can work on your handheld during your flight. Take this time away from the grid to go in and organize everything. Erase any unneeded messages from your inbox, clear any drafts you might have saved, delete old voice mail messages, and update your contacts.

Your laptop is another technological quagmire of files and messages and all sorts of other stuff that needs filing, deleting, and updating. Again, as long as you turn your wireless off, it's okay to operate your laptop while on the plane. Go through and delete old files, make accessible folders for your most important documents, and cycle through and erase old message from your Outlook or Entourage.

432
Organize your laptop.

When was the last time you had some time to play with the features of Word? A lot of the time, you're taking extra steps to accomplish something in the program that one of its many features will automatically do for you. Take some time and play around with Word and the other programs in the Office Suite. This will definitely help your productivity once you return to the office.

433
Increase your Word skills.

Some people are very familiar with Excel. Others find themselves very lost whenever they open up one of its spreadsheets. If you're in the latter group, use your flight to walk through the tutorial that Excel offers. Learn how to manipulate cells and have the program run summations for you. Again, these tips will aid your office productivity.

434
Increase your Excel skills.

435
How do you deal with conflict?

When a conflict arises in your office, do you fight it, flee, or try to talk things out? The manner in which you respond to inner or outer pressure tells other people—such as employers and employees—the content of your character. If your seatmates are game, try out different conflict strategies by role-playing. What do you find yourself feeling led to do? Is it the best thing? Could another method of conflict resolution be more successful?

436
Develop a mission statement.

A mission statement sums up the company's beliefs in a reasonably short maxim. Make up your own mission statement. If you own your business, create one for that. If you run a department within a company, draft one for all your direct reports. If you're just in charge of you, develop a personal mission statement applicable to your position. Remind yourself of this every day. It will come in handy during performance reviews.

437
Take your company green.

Global warming has become a favorite American cause. The gas-guzzling SUVs and "live for today, who cares about tomorrow" lifestyle have led us, some say, to the brink of catastrophe. Brainstorm ways that your office can be ecologically sensitive. Waste paper on needless copies and memos? See if your company would be willing to go paperless—bringing laptops to meetings and accessing files from there and circulating memos via e-mail.

If you want to get ahead in your profession, you've got to present major-league projects to your boss. Now that you've got time, brainstorm projects that will sweep your boss off his feet. Think about things he has said, such as "I wish we had someone who knew something about time-management strategies." If he's made it clear what he'd like to see, how can you give him what he wants? The key to success is making your boss's job easier.

438
Plan out work projects.

If you're at the entry level in your profession, you may not even have considered retirement yet. After all, it's so far away. But keep in mind that the days of pensions are drawing to a close. Make a note to enroll in your company's 401(k) plan. Get some information about IRAs (individual retirement accounts) and read up on various plans during your flight. The earlier you start saving, the better off you'll be.

439
Consider retirement.

Even if you've just started in your company and feel you'll be happy merely to survive the first year, you should not discount your potential for leadership. Write a list of the qualities you believe exemplify a good manager. How many do you have? How many do you think you could acquire? How many do you think you could never acquire in a million years? What can you do to build your strengths and remedy your weaknesses?

440
What becomes a manager most?

441
Develop a foolproof advertising campaign.

Whether or not you're in advertising or marketing, come up with a way to market one of your company's products or services. Most commercials are so lame, you wonder how they could possibly make anybody want to buy what they're selling. You could do better, of course. Use your time to come up with the next "Where's the beef" or "HeadOn: Apply directly to the forehead. HeadOn: Apply directly to the forehead. HeadOn: Apply directly to the forehead."

442
Plan an office fundraiser for a charity.

Think of a unique way to raise money for a good cause. Brainstorm ideas. Once you have some good ones, plot out the materials and manpower you would need to make the ideas a reality. When you get back to the office, share your idea with your coworkers and see who would be game to help you out.

443
Start a blog.

While you won't be able to launch your blog on the plane due to the lack of wireless Internet, you can certainly start coming up with content. If you're a small business owner, entrepreneur, or author, a blog is an inexpensive way to get some publicity. The more attention you can bring to your product or service, the better.

It's a dog-eat-dog world characterized by rats racing. Be ruthless. How could you make sure your product is preferred over your competitors'? Think about it. Make it a sport. Even if you don't follow through on your ideas, you will feel better after coming up with some good, juicy ways to screw the competition.

444
How can you screw the competition?

Back in the days of pillaging and plundering, pirates would hold a mutiny onboard any ship that was being led by a captain who was only looking out for his best interest. Do you have that type of "captain" leading your "ship"? If so, mutiny! Of course, it won't include his walking the plank, but if you talk with other unsatisfied employees and present a united front of disapproval to his manager or Human Resources, you may get the ball rolling.

445
Lead an office revolt.

Every company looks to innovate. Now that you have time to think about your work, recognize a challenge that your department is facing. Or think of an out-of-date practice that everyone seems complacent with performing. What are solutions to this problem? Come up with a clear plan on how to move in a new direction. Type up your plan and set up a meeting with your manager. Explain your idea and bask in the (hopefully) pending accolades.

446
Be an innovator.

447
Work on your resume.

If you're unsatisfied with your job, or feel that it's time to move on, start looking for places that offer opportunities that interest you. However, in order to act on these opportunities, you need to have a solid resume prepared. Take this opportunity that your flight has presented to call up your resume on your computer. Freshen it up. Revise your current job description with any new duties and add any recent achievements.

448
Network.

Be sure to slip some of your business cards into your wallet or purse before you head to the airport. You never know whom you'll be sitting next to on the plane and how they could positively affect your career. Start up a friendly chat with your seatmates and see what they do for a living. If it's something that crosses paths with your field, offer to exchange business cards.

449
Plan your professional future.

The last thing you want to do when you leave work is to think about work. That's why so many people wind up unhappy with their jobs, doing the same thing day after day. Don't fall into that trap! You have some time now to really think about what you want to do with your life and where you need to be in order to accomplish those goals. Come up with a timeline for your career with achievable benchmarks at set intervals.

"If you don't give me X, Y, and Z, then I quit!" Figure out what's really important to your career happiness and fill in X, Y, and Z. Then resolve that you are going to meet with your manager when you return to your office and make him meet your demands, or you'll hand in your walking papers.

450

Decide on an ultimatum—and stick to it.

RELIGIOUS
EXPERIENCE

Soaring through the clouds, lifted into the sky, on your way to a final destination ... it just lends itself to a religious experience—or LSD trip. Whether you pray to God, look to Mohammed, bow to the Buddha, or praise Vishnu, the chance to reflect on your religion and those of others is a worthwhile experience. And since you have a while before touchdown, why not take a chance to do it now?

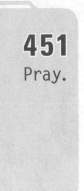

451
Pray.

If you haven't spoken to God in a while, now is the time. You can drop the formal "thees" and "thous." Just talk to God— however you envision God—as you would a close friend. Speak about your concerns and fears. Ask for guidance and wisdom. Odds are, by the time you land, you'll feel a newfound sense of direction.

452
Pick a mantra.

The mantra is the cornerstone of Eastern religion. All the cool people have one: a special series of syllables that puts them into a state of deep relaxation. Pick a mantra and let it resonate in your head throughout the flight. It will calm you in the event of turbulence.

453
Focus on your chakras.

According to New Age religions, chakras are seven energy centers in the body. Each of these centers can be opened if you lay the right color crystal on them. Put violet on the top of your head, indigo on your brow, blue on your throat, green on your heart, yellow on your solar plexus, orange on your navel, and red on your sacrum. Other folks will think you're crazy, but you'll be filled with so much positive energy that you won't care.

It will make you feel better. Draw a picture of your boss, your ex, or some other unpleasant person. Make the likeness as realistic as possible. Then, once you're done, draw little *x*'s on various parts of the figure's body. Give him sore knees. Give her a headache. Delight in making him or her miserable.

454
Practice some minor voodoo.

Some saints and other supremely holy folks are said to rise into the air, seemingly on their own power. Now that you're in the air—through no effort of your own—concentrate and try to rise up out of your seat. Focusing on such a goal may seem silly (Ok, *is* silly), but it is also quite calming. Imagine yourself rising above the rest of your seatmates. Then maybe you won't be so annoyed by the armrest hog next to you.

455
Try to levitate.

What does God look like to you? Is he a benevolent old man with a long, white beard? Is she a goddess with a golden gown? Is it a ray of shimmering light that pierces all darkness? Focus on your own conception of God, and let that vision soothe and comfort you during your flight.

456
Envision the face of God.

457
Wipe out your seven deadly sins.

All of us combat some of the seven deadly sins: pride, envy, wrath, sloth, avarice, gluttony, and lust. Which ones do you struggle with most? What can you do to lessen their grips on you? Make a plan to expel the seven deadly sins from your life.

458
Call on your personal angel.

Remember Clarence, the guardian angel who saved the life of George Bailey in *It's a Wonderful Life*? You might have your own Clarence. Angels are ethereal beings said to float invisibly about us. Some believe they are agents of God who bring peace and healing to those with faith in a higher power. Find that faith within yourself and call on your own personal angel to bring you comfort and an end to your problems.

459
Have you ever witnessed a miracle?

Discuss miracles with your seatmates. Chances are, you've experienced coincidences or odd events that you can't explain, events that turned out to make a positive difference in your life. Do miracles exist? Find out what others have experienced. Talk about your own encounters with the miraculous.

Every religion in the world has a different take on the end times. What's yours? According to speculation based on the Mayan calendar, the end of the world is scheduled for sometime in 2012. Write down everything you want to do before it's humanity's curtain call. (If you're reading this in the future and the 2012-hype panned out to be as real as Y2K, feel free to laugh.)

460
It's the apocalypse— *run!*

If science fiction writer L. Ron Hubbard could do it, why can't you? Hubbard created Scientology, which has become the faith of many celebrities. Simply think of some lofty-sounding goals, such as spiritual improvement or communion with the Oversoul. Then come up with some gobbledygook that will help people achieve those goals. Maybe, someday, you'll have A-list stars practicing Bobology or whatever you choose to call your new religion.

461
Create your own religion.

Think about your parents' religion and their religious practices. How do they compare to yours? Are they Buddhists, while you've become a conservative Christian? How and why did that happen? Take your time in the sky to contemplate and reevaluate your decisions.

462
Reflect on your religious path.

463
Learn about another religion.

Most Americans are Christians, and Christianity is the world's largest religion. But there are many other faiths to learn about. Pick up a book at the library on Islam, Judaism, Buddhism, or a Christian denomination you're unfamiliar with. Read through and see how this other religion differs from yours.

464
Confucius says ...

Confucius is still considered one of the wisest people in history. The Chinese sage died more than 2,500 years ago, but his wisdom lives on in the *Analects*. The *Analects* do not offer practical advice per se; instead, they force you to think critically about important matters. By "rewiring" your brain, the *Analects* can help you think creatively, potentially a great boon for your employment security.

465
Muse over Zen koans.

What's the sound of one hand clapping? What is your original face before you were born? Does a dog have Buddha-nature? These age-old meditation prompts are meant to get you thinking outside the box and on a higher plane of being. Concentrate on the question at hand and maybe you will achieve superior enlightenment before you arrive at your destination.

Regardless of your religious persuasion, the Holy Bible is a corking read, complete with all manner of battles, bloodshed, and dangerous liaisons. And that's just the first three or four books! The New Testament, by contrast, is filled with love and forgiveness. Whatever your mood, the Bible is bound to satisfy ... and it's one of the unofficial pillars of our Judeo-Christian society.

466
Study the Bible.

The Christian Old Testament's Book of Exodus (20:2–17) contains the most famous set of rules in history: the Ten Commandments. How many of them do you actually know? How many of them do you routinely break? How could it change your life if you took them to heart?

467
Learn the Ten Commandments.

Pop star Madonna, actress Demi Moore, and comedienne Roseanne Barr are only three celebrities who swear by the kabbalah. It's a body of mystical Hebrew teachings, based on interpretations of the Hebrew scriptures. Thanks to its adoption by celebrities, plenty of books on the kabbalah are in circulation. Pick one up and see what all the fuss is about.

468
Study the kabbalah.

469
Study the Upanishads.

The Upanishads compose a sacred Hindu text that focuses on the nature of human-kind and its relationship to a formless "ultimate soul" called Brahman that is roughly equivalent to the Christian God. In essence, the Upanishads seek to show that your soul and Brahman are one and the same. Whatever your faith, the Upanishads can give you a glimpse into the wisdom of people who worshiped hundreds of years before the birth of Christ.

470
Read the Bhagavad-Gita.

The Bhagavad-Gita, which translates roughly to "Song of the Divine One," is sort of like the Hindu Bible. The Gita, as it is commonly known, is in the form of a conversation between Krishna—think of him as equivalent to God in Western traditions—and a hero named Arjuna. Their conversation details the basic philosophy of the Hindu tradition.

471
Read the Popol Vuh.

Indigenous societies thrived in the Americas long before Europeans arrived. One of these, the Mayans of Guatemala, based their lives on the Popol Vuh, or "Book of the Community." The manuscript contains the Mayan creation myth as well as other mythological stories. It's a fascinating glimpse of the pre-Columbian (i.e., before Columbus) Meso-American (roughly Central American) world.

Pope Gregory may or may not have developed the chant that bears his name, but it hardly matters. Since the tenth century of the Common Era, pious clergy have sung these simple, monophonic (meaning they are sung without harmonies) songs of devotion. Gregorian chants have the same purpose as mantras in Eastern religious traditions. Listen to an album of chants and let the music whisk you to a higher spiritual plane.

472
Listen to Gregorian chants.

This is the "Traveler's Prayer" and is recited by many Jewish people when they travel: "May it be Your will, LORD, our God and the God of our ancestors, that You lead us toward peace, guide our footsteps toward peace, and make us reach our desired destination for life, gladness, and peace. May You hear the sound of our humble request because You are God Who hears prayer requests. Blessed are You, Adonai, Who hears prayer."

473
Recite the Tefilat HaDerech.

One of the most important tenets of Islam is that all believers make a pilgrimage to Mecca. However, a religious pilgrimage can apply to a variety of other beliefs, and it's an important and influential spiritual journey. These trips have the ability to reaffirm your faith and heighten the appreciation you have for your religion. Spend your time onboard identifying the site you should visit and planning out a trip to this holy destination.

474
Plan a pilgrimage.

REBUS PUZZLES

So you think you're smart because you figured out where your layover terminal was in relation to where your original flight landed? Good for you! You can really put your smarts to the test with these teasers. In order to decode a common word or phrase, you must decipher the unusual placement of letters and words in the puzzle. The answers are in the back of the book for when you give up.

475
Rebus Puzzle #1

STRUmusicalMENTS

ANSWER: _____

476
Rebus Puzzle #2

YOU JUST ME

ANSWER: _____

477
Rebus Puzzle #3

Beatles
Titanic

ANSWER: _____

478
Rebus Puzzle #4

+ ´

ANSWER: _____

479
Rebus Puzzle #5

GRH2OAH2OVE

ANSWER: _____

HICANS

ANSWER: _____

480
Rebus Puzzle #6

ECNALG

ANSWER: _____

481
Rebus Puzzle #7

EAREAR

ANSWER: _____

482
Rebus Puzzle #8

O_ER_T_O_

ANSWER: _____

483
Rebus Puzzle #9

ENTURY

ANSWER: _____

484
Rebus Puzzle #10

485
Rebus Puzzle #11

STEP PETS PETS

ANSWER: _____

486
Rebus Puzzle #12

cHIMp

ANSWER: _____

487
Rebus Puzzle #13

IGAR, CIGR, CGAR, CIGA, CIAR

ANSWER: _____

488
Rebus Puzzle #14

JOBINJOB

ANSWER: _____

489
Rebus Puzzle #15

NOSE
$$$
CHIN

ANSWER: _____

eyee cexcept

ANSWER: _____

490
Rebus Puzzle #16

Close Close Comfort Comfort Comfort Comfort

ANSWER: _____

491
Rebus Puzzle #17

VA DERS

ANSWER: _____

492
Rebus Puzzle #18

Guyyyy

ANSWER: _____

493
Rebus Puzzle #19

SEcu4rE

ANSWER: _____

494
Rebus Puzzle #20

495
Rebus Puzzle #21

biddenbiddenbiddenbiddenfruit

ANSWER: _____

496
Rebus Puzzle #22

smupoke

ANSWER: _____

497
Rebus Puzzle #23

getgetitgetget

ANSWER: _____

498
Rebus Puzzle #24

KNOWITNO

ANSWER: _____

499
Rebus Puzzle #25

Cont_ol

ANSWER: _____

Dinner and a movie
    Leg

ANSWER: _____

500
Rebus Puzzle #26

NE
RV
OU
 S

ANSWER: _____

501
Rebus Puzzle #27

PICT RES

ANSWER: _____

502
Rebus Puzzle #28

---

sssssssssse

ANSWER: _____

503
Rebus Puzzle #29

CCCCCCC

ANSWER: _____

504
Rebus Puzzle #30

RHYME TIME

Keep your brain sharp with these Seussian puzzles that will have you speaking in rhyme and a singsong pattern all the way to your destination. Each clue leads you to a rhyming word pair. If anything, these are a great warm-up for *Jeopardy!*—Trebek loves his "Rhyme Time" category.

505
Rhyme Time
Puzzle #1

Leisurely moving a boat

ANSWER: _____

506
Rhyme Time
Puzzle #2

The correct evening

ANSWER: _____

507
Rhyme Time
Puzzle #3

Fear in the barbershop

ANSWER: _____

508
Rhyme Time
Puzzle #4

A shy lad

ANSWER: _____

509
Rhyme Time
Puzzle #5

Sixty minutes of rain

ANSWER: _____

510
Rhyme Time
Puzzle #6

A reptile genius

ANSWER: _____

A very strange rock-and-roll instrument

ANSWER: _____

511
Rhyme Time
Puzzle #7

The main robber

ANSWER: _____

512
Rhyme Time
Puzzle #8

A not-so-intelligent matchmaker

ANSWER: _____

513
Rhyme Time
Puzzle #9

An unpleasant matriarch

ANSWER: _____

514
Rhyme Time
Puzzle #10

A wonderful spouse

ANSWER: _____

515
Rhyme Time
Puzzle #11

An inexpensive sound

ANSWER: _____

516
Rhyme Time
Puzzle #12

517
Rhyme Time
Puzzle #13

A passageway for giants

ANSWER: _____

518
Rhyme Time
Puzzle #14

A choral program after winter

ANSWER: _____

519
Rhyme Time
Puzzle #15

A disorganized game

ANSWER: _____

520
Rhyme Time
Puzzle #16

A special bucket deal

ANSWER: _____

521
Rhyme Time
Puzzle #17

A tidy road

ANSWER: _____

522
Rhyme Time
Puzzle #18

Burning rubber

ANSWER: _____

A utensil for dried plums

ANSWER: _____

523
Rhyme Time
Puzzle #19

A large gulp

ANSWER: _____

524
Rhyme Time
Puzzle #20

An animal dance

ANSWER: _____

525
Rhyme Time
Puzzle #21

A ten-cent citrus

ANSWER: _____

526
Rhyme Time
Puzzle #22

An oversized head covering

ANSWER: _____

527
Rhyme Time
Puzzle #23

A sturdy piece of furniture

ANSWER: _____

528
Rhyme Time
Puzzle #24

529
Rhyme Time
Puzzle #25

A silent woodwind

ANSWER: _____

530
Rhyme Time
Puzzle #26

Courteous members of the rodent family

ANSWER: _____

531
Rhyme Time
Puzzle #27

The top guest

ANSWER: _____

532
Rhyme Time
Puzzle #28

A snowed-in vehicle

ANSWER: _____

533
Rhyme Time
Puzzle #29

A roll to go with your burnt burger

ANSWER: _____

534
Rhyme Time
Puzzle #30

A lone security guard

ANSWER: _____

An ant's punch

ANSWER: _____

535

A sunburned bald man

ANSWER: _____

536

A short-term fire starter

ANSWER: _____

537

A spinal exam

ANSWER: _____

538

It's your time to shine

ANSWER: _____

539

Post-performance direction

ANSWER: _____

540

ODD ONE OUT

Remember *Sesame Street* and its "which one of these things doesn't belong" segment? Of course you do. This section of puzzles will keep you from fading during your flight, as it calls on this same method of distinction. Read through the list of words and choose the one that doesn't fit with the others. While it's a little more challenging than Big Bird's version, it'll keep you just as entertained.

541
Odd One Out
Puzzle #1

Which word does not belong: pear, hen, apple, ring, turtle *Hint:* It is definitely a seasonal item.

ANSWER:_____

542
Odd One Out
Puzzle #2

Which word does not belong: ketchup, mustard, soy sauce, dressing, barbecue sauce *Hint:* The colder, the better.

ANSWER:_____

543
Odd One Out
Puzzle #3

Which word does not belong: Maine, California, New York, Wyoming *Hint:* The cities are also important.

ANSWER:_____

544
Odd One Out
Puzzle #4

Which word does not belong: date, rage, wear, pale, west *Hint:* Try to use your hands.

ANSWER:_____

545
Odd One Out
Puzzle #5

Which word does not belong: Paris, Rome, New York, Milan, Sydney *Hint:* Demographics play no part.

ANSWER:_____

546
Odd One Out
Puzzle #6

Which word does not belong: bell, jump, chat, door, bed *Hint:* It is often found in school classrooms.

ANSWER:_____

Which word does not belong: canary, dog, parrot, rabbit, hamster, pony *Hint:* The family name is important to this puzzle.

ANSWER: _____

547
Odd One Out
Puzzle #7

Which word does not belong: liberty, venture, loyal, conquest, escape, endeavor *Hint:* You can drive yourself crazy with this.

ANSWER: _____

548
Odd One Out
Puzzle #8

Which word does not belong: start, sharp, crazy, land, sofa *Hint:* At the end of the lane you might find an answer.

ANSWER: _____

549
Odd One Out
Puzzle #9

Which word does not belong: bread, cover, trail, trade, friend
Hint: The letter *e* is not the answer.

ANSWER: _____

550
Odd One Out
Puzzle #10

Which word does not belong: Daniel, Jacob, Michael, John, Robert *Hint:* Do not look to the Bible for a solution here.

ANSWER: _____

551
Odd One Out
Puzzle #11

Which word does not belong: red, green, purple, brown, blue *Hint:* Hopefully something will give you a sign.

ANSWER: _____

552
Odd One Out
Puzzle #12

553
Odd One Out
Puzzle #13

Which letter does not belong in this group: a, t, f, r, z *Hint:* Pay attention to the right pieces.

ANSWER: _____

554
Odd One Out
Puzzle #14

Which word does not belong: bull, fish, lion, giraffe, crab *Hint:* You might be drawn to one choice over another.

ANSWER: _____

555
Odd One Out
Puzzle #15

Which word does not belong: tired, shy, jealous, delighted, sullen *Hint:* Childish innocence will help you figure this out.

ANSWER: _____

556
Odd One Out
Puzzle #16

Which word does not belong: knowledge, family, time, career, creativity *Hint:* You can bring these items into focus.

ANSWER: _____

557
Odd One Out
Puzzle #17

Which word does not belong: horn, doll, teddy, drum, elephant, boat *Hint:* Children love these types of toys as gifts.

ANSWER: _____

558
Odd One Out
Puzzle #18

Which word does not belong: Henry, Romeo, Hamlet, John, Richard *Hint:* The role is equally as important.

ANSWER: _____

Which word does not belong: apricot, melon, orange, plum, apple *Hint:* The scents were never appreciated.

559

ANSWER: _____

Which word does not belong: rabbit, buffalo, elephant, goat, dog, pig *Hint:* Lucky animals who got called to a meeting.

560

ANSWER: _____

Which word does not belong: elf, sole, rose, sofa, moon, donkey, pink *Hint:* They attempt to be educational.

561

ANSWER: _____

Which word does not belong: Capella, Altair, Regulus, Jasper, Castor, Shaula *Hint:* Heavy names for a light topic.

562

ANSWER: _____

Which word does not belong: awake, Zen, calm, energy, passion, refresh *Hint:* They do exactly what they say.

563

ANSWER: _____

Which word does not belong: California, New York, Ohio, Texas, Florida *Hint:* Location is not so imperative.

564

ANSWER: _____

565
Odd One Out
Puzzle #25

Which word does not belong: California,
New York, Texas, New Mexico, Montana
Hint: The area you live in is important.

ANSWER: _____

566
Odd One Out
Puzzle #26

Which word does not belong: California,
New York, Florida, Texas, Illinois
Hint: Are you sick of dealing with states?

ANSWER: _____

567
Odd One Out
Puzzle #27

Which word does not belong: Stone,
Steve, Ed, Tim, Joseph *Hint:* These names
require some character development.

ANSWER: _____

568
Odd One Out
Puzzle #28

Which word does not belong:
Moscow, Sydney, Tokyo, Toronto, Rome
Hint: It will not get quite as crowded.

ANSWER: _____

569
Odd One Out
Puzzle #29

Which word does not belong: Switzerland, Belgium, Canada, Denmark, Spain
Hint: They have their reasons.

ANSWER: _____

570
Odd One Out
Puzzle #30

Which does not belong: *The Godfather, Peggy
Sue Got Married, The Outsiders, Finian's Rainbow,
The Great Gatsby Hint:* One name unites them.

ANSWER: _____

Which word does not belong: heat, magic, jazz, dance, sun *Hint:* It can get quite hot when they get going.

ANSWER: _____

571
Odd One Out
Puzzle #31

Which word does not belong: sneakers, trucks, eyeglasses, popsy, dedication *Hint:* A collection worth having.

ANSWER: _____

572
Odd One Out
Puzzle #32

Which word does not belong: pirate, glacier, arches, olympic, voyageurs *Hint:* It is time for a camping trip.

ANSWER: _____

573
Odd One Out
Puzzle #33

Which word does not belong: Exxon, Ford, Chevron, General Motors, Chrysler *Hint:* Some do better than others.

ANSWER: _____

574
Odd One Out
Puzzle #34

Which word does not belong: tart, top, kite, hoe, low *Hint:* Each word has a beginning and an end.

ANSWER: _____

575
Odd One Out
Puzzle #35

Which word does not belong: pots, reed, tram, poor, ward *Hint:* An interesting way to read.

ANSWER: _____

576
Odd One Out
Puzzle #36

577
Odd One Out
Puzzle #37

Which word does not belong: cleave, assume, crime, dust, skin *Hint:* It depends on the context of the sentence.

ANSWER: _____

578
Odd One Out
Puzzle #38

Which word does not belong: falcons, jets, condors, ravens, seahawks *Hint:* The fact that they can fly is irrelevant.

ANSWER: _____

579
Odd One Out
Puzzle #39

Which word does not belong: choir, dreams, criticism, hymn, serenade *Hint:* You might need to read further into the choices.

ANSWER: _____

580
Odd One Out
Puzzle #40

Which does not belong: Arabian oryx, hump-head wrasse, golden lion tamarin, gopher tortoises, black-footed ferret *Hint:* So few left.

ANSWER: _____

581
Odd One Out
Puzzle #41

Which word does not belong: band, sing, aisle, chants, choir *Hint:* English class comes in handy.

ANSWER: _____

582
Odd One Out
Puzzle #42

Which word does not belong: bloomer, volt, watt, bulb, saxophone *Hint:* An interesting spin on the name of the words.

ANSWER: _____

Which word does not belong:
display, buffet, minute, accent, present
Hint: I think I know what you're saying.
ANSWER: _____

583
Odd One Out
Puzzle #43

Which word does not belong:
travel, vagrant, chant, agile, needles
Hint: It is a betting favorite.
ANSWER: _____

584
Odd One Out
Puzzle #44

Which word does not belong:
pioneer, Hudson, Galileo, Viking, Magellan
Hint: The answer involves expeditions.
ANSWER: _____

585
Odd One Out
Puzzle #45

Which word does not belong:
cat, dog, lion, sheep, horse, lamb
Hint: It was left out on purpose.
ANSWER: _____

586
Odd One Out
Puzzle #46

Which word does not belong:
play, skip, hope, care, youth
Hint: A little bit of math is necessary.
ANSWER: _____

587
Odd One Out
Puzzle #47

Which word does not belong:
Sappers, Cells, Treasure, Loot, Mandalay
Hint: An early nineteenth-century solution.
ANSWER: _____

588
Odd One Out
Puzzle #48

589
Odd One Out
Puzzle #49

Which word does not belong:
cat, ladder, key, salt, eyelash
Hint: Be careful with your choice.

ANSWER: _____

590
Odd One Out
Puzzle #50

Which word does not belong: Nigeria,
Angola, Italy, Ireland, Germany
Hint: Keep your thoughts in alignment.

ANSWER: _____

591
Odd One Out
Puzzle #51

Which word does not belong:
star, planet, sun, tree, bear
Hint: Show your pride and heritage.

ANSWER: _____

592
Odd One Out
Puzzle #52

Which word does not belong:
man, win, vent, wing, cake, key
Hint: Start off with a bit of geography.

ANSWER: _____

593
Odd One Out
Puzzle #53

Which word does not belong:
taste, chocolate, flash, legs, splash, spot
Hint: A collector's more recent find.

ANSWER: _____

594
Odd One Out
Puzzle #54

Which word does not belong:
butt, pipe, firkin, double, runlet
Hint: Let's make a toast.

ANSWER: _____

Which word does not belong: fool, devil, tower, sun, world, justice, castle *Hint:* Years ago the answer would remain the same.

ANSWER: _____

595
Odd One Out
Puzzle #55

Which word does not belong: Alice, celebrity, bananas, Manhattan, beach, September *Hint:* Part of the puzzle wore many hats.

ANSWER: _____

596
Odd One Out
Puzzle #56

Which word does not belong: best, square, tall, final, whole, mortal *Hint:* One of the toughest puzzles in the bunch.

ANSWER: _____

597
Odd One Out
Puzzle #57

Which word does not belong: news, goods, phonics, mathematics, civics, billiards *Hint:* Look at the words one time.

ANSWER: _____

598
Odd One Out
Puzzle #58

Which word does not belong: table, stool, eat, jump, silver *Hint:* Jump and bump.

ANSWER: _____

599
Odd One Out
Puzzle #59

Which word does not belong: balk, boot, chair, fall, net, sin, stable *Hint:* You may need a sporting chance.

ANSWER: _____

600
Odd One Out
Puzzle #60

SUGGESTED READING

A great mainstay in in-flight entertainment is reading. Most people don't have the chance to just sit, relax, and enjoy a good book unless they are traveling. However, at times the problem isn't whether to read, but what to read. To answer that quandary, here's a suggested reading list that will have the pages and miles flying by. Grab a copy of whatever piques your interest for the return flight, or snatch up a copy at the terminal's bookstore during your layover.

601
Read a book on personal finance.

If you're one of those people who doesn't have a clue how to handle their money, you have plenty of company. That's why thousands of books on personal finance exist. Before your flight, find one of these books that seems suitable for you. Bring it with you, and force yourself to read about a subject that may stress you out. When you return to earth, put into practice what you've learned.

602
Read a literary classic.

Enjoying the classics of literature is in danger of becoming a lost art in this age of popular fiction and hyped books. Think of a book that you skipped over in high school or college and revisit it on your plane ride. You may appreciate a work like *Pride and Prejudice*, *Anna Karenina*, or *The Brothers Karamazov* now more than ever.

603
Actually read *Playboy*.

Since it debuted in 1953, the standard response a boy or man gives when caught with a *Playboy* is to claim: "I'm just reading it for the articles." In fact, the magazine always has prided itself—and rightly so—on the quality of its articles, interviews, and fiction. Dare to bring *Playboy* onto the plane ... and actually *read* it.

Hell was never so cool as when Italian poet Dante Alighieri took readers on a tour of it in *The Divine Comedy*. It begins in hell, continues through purgatory, and ends in paradise ... hence it has a happy ending and qualifies as a comedy. Only scholars read the last two works. But anyone can enjoy *Inferno*, Dante's depiction of a hell ruled over by a three-headed Satan. The tortures Dante describes continue to show up in modern Hollywood slasher films.

604
Explore Dante's *Inferno*.

Prior to your flight, track down a copy of one of Shakespeare's plays and find a soliloquy. Just pick a play, choose a main character, and scan the text for a very long speech by that character. The last stipulation is that the speech be given while alone, or out of earshot of any other characters. (Try *Othello* or *Macbeth* for an easy find.) Use your flight to read over the soliloquy, memorize it, and recite it.

605
Memorize one of Shakespeare's soliloquies.

OK, so this technically is cheating, but if you're not much of a reader, you might prefer a book on compact disc. Most new books are available in this format. Not only do you get the story—complete in some cases with sound effects—but having it read to you will help take your mind off of cramped space, turbulence, and other unpleasant flight issues.

606
Listen to a book on CD.

607

Read a banned book.

Name a popular, long-enjoyed book, and it probably has been banned at one time or another. So be a literary badass and pick up a banned book. You can find a good list of banned books at *http://digital.library.upenn.edu/books/banned-books.html*. Find one that sounds appealing to you, grab a copy before you board, and spend your flight supporting free speech.

608

Read popular fiction.

If you consider yourself an intellectual, it's time for you to get into the gutter with a popular, mass-market paperback. Dare to read Jackie Collins, Tom Clancy, or John Grisham. Even if plot-driven fiction leaves you cold, it will still keep you turning pages.

609

Read a nonfiction children's book.

Let's say you don't know anything about biology. You don't know photosynthesis from photographs of Paris Hilton. You're an intellectual, and you like to learn, but you just can't face a 500-page book on biology. Don't despair. Pick up a children's nonfiction book at your local bookstore or library. These volumes are designed to be simple and straightforward. You'll land in Des Moines ten times smarter than you were when you took off from La Guardia.

As you have aged, you have become more sophisticated. The same is true for the comic books you grew up with. Many familiar titles still exist, but you'll barely recognize your old heroes if you haven't picked up a comic book in decades. Illustrations have risen to high-art status. Situations have become increasingly gritty and realistic. Pick up titles you used to love, and see what your favorite characters are up to these days.

610
Revisit comic books.

These are books you probably gave a look past when you were a youth. But revisiting them now will allow you to uncover some wisdom and truth the author hid within his sing-songy, rhyming works. Grab a copy of *The Cat in the Hat*, *Green Eggs and Ham*, or *Oh, the Places You'll Go* for an airplane ride full of laughs and inspiration.

611
Peruse some Dr. Seuss.

Now that J. K. Rowling has completed all the books within her series about the heroic boy wizard, Harry Potter, see what all the fuss is about. If you have any spirit of adventure and imagination, you'll be hooked. And the good news for you is that you won't have to suffer through the wait for the next book's release as many Potter fans dealt with as they read while Rowling finished writing.

612
Catch *Potter*-fever.

613
Begin *Don Quixote.*

Miguel de Cervantes's *Don Quixote* is considered one of the first novels. Published in 1605, the Spanish novelist's work follows Don Quixote, a crazy old man who decides he is a noble knight. His "adventures" tend to end in disaster. *Don Quixote* is a picaresque novel, which means it contains a series of adventures. Think of them as episodes of a television show. You can start anywhere in the novel and read whichever sections you like.

614
Read foreign literature.

If you are an American, chances are you don't read much world literature. Rectify that missing piece of your intellectual life while on your transcontinental flight. Use the following Web link to read a great list of world authors whose books you can find at your local library or bookstore: *www .dmozorg/Arts/Literature/World_Literature.*

615
Read some armchair travel.

"Armchair travel" is a genre of books for folks who like to read about exotic places but who would rather remain in the suburbs. Now that you actually are going somewhere, you may as well give yourself the surreal experience of reading a travel account as you yourself travel.

All kinds of household hints and tips books that can help you save thousands on simple home repairs. Pick one up and learn what to do the next time a faucet starts spouting off, your doorbell stops letting you ring its bells, or you find yourself in the gutter ... trying desperately to remove leaves from it.

616
Read a D-I-Y guide.

Although it can seem old-fashioned, William Shakespeare wrote in modern English—the same language you use today. Geoffrey Chaucer, on the other hand, is the real deal. His immortal *Canterbury Tales*, which follows a group of zany pilgrims to a saint's shrine, is in Middle English. Try reading it that way. It's challenging, but not impossible, and it will give you insights into the origins of today's English.

617
Read *The Canterbury Tales* in Middle English.

A roman à clef (pronounced roh-MAHN ah-CLAY) is a novel that focuses on real-life events while fictionalizing them slightly. Some great works of fiction are romans à clef: Hemingway's *The Sun Also Rises*, nearly all of Jack Kerouac's novels, Sylvia Plath's *The Bell Jar*, and, more recently, Lauren Weisberger's *The Devil Wears Prada* is a roman à clef about the author's days as an intern at *Vogue* magazine.

618
Read a roman à clef.

619
Read an epic poem.

Epic poems are one of literature's oldest forms. Essentially, they are very long narrative poems that tell stories about characters who are larger than life. Ancient epics include Homer's *Odyssey* and *Iliad* and the *Epic of Gilgamesh*. You might try John Milton's epic *Paradise Lost,* about the "birth" of Satan. Finally, you could choose a modern epic such as Ezra Pound's *Cantos* or William Carlos Williams's *Paterson*.

620
Reread your favorite book.

Be sure to pack that dog-eared copy of your favorite book. A favorite deserves rereading as many times as possible. This allows you to really get a sense of the book, its characters, and its purpose. As you reread it this time onboard the plane, approach it from a different perspective or with a set of questions. Is the protagonist really as heroic as you first thought? Is the antagonist really *that* evil?

621
Reread your least favorite book.

This sounds like a painful exercise in literature appreciation; however, it can be an eye-opening experience. The way you perceive a book upon first reading is often dependent on where you are in your life at that point. You inflect your knowledge and current disposition on the conflicts and characters. So rereading a book you immediately dismissed as awful gives it another chance now that you've had the opportunity to grow and change.

Look around and see if anyone else has a book they're just not that into. Offer up a proposition: your book for theirs. If they take advantage of the miles-high swap, you have an opportunity to read something you may never have thought of picking up. If they scoff at your suggestion, leave them be with a muffled *bah humbug*.

622
Swap books with a fellow traveler.

The board members at the Modern Library have released a list of what they believe to be the 100 Best Novels. Make sure they've completed the list. Visit the Modern Library's Web site (*www.modernlibrary .com*) and your local bookstore before your flight to begin your trek through the greatest. Just for conversation's sake, their top five in order are: *Ulysses*, *The Great Gatsby*, *A Portrait of the Artist as a Young Man*, *Lolita*, and *Brave New World*.

623
Tackle the greatest novels of all time.

You've "mistakenly" walked down this aisle while shuffling around the bookstore, checking out the titles and seeing if any apply to the number of problems you're facing in your life. Well, now is the perfect time to "mistakenly" buy one and "mistakenly" pack it in your carry-on, so you can "mistakenly" read it where no one you can see you.

624
Read a self-help book.

625
The movie's better.

More often than not, whenever a book is made into a movie there is a unanimous response that the book is *so* much better. However, sometimes there is that rare occurrence where the onscreen adaptation surpasses the literary work on which it's based. Pick up one of the following books—*Jaws*, *Forrest Gump*, or *Sideways*—read it on your flight, and then rent the movie and judge for yourself.

626
Catch up with Jane.

Austen-lovers have always been large in number, but it seems that there's been an even greater surge in her popularity as of late. Take one of her romances onboard and lose yourself in her beautiful prose. Whether you choose a classic like *Sense and Sensibility* or *Emma*, or opt for one of her posthumous works, *Persuasion* or *Northanger Abbey*, you're guaranteed a great read.

627
Read an author who's your opposite.

People often gravitate to authors who are seemingly similar to them. There's an approachability and comfort that comes from knowing the person who's crafted this story is similar to you, the reader. Break out of that comfort zone. Find an author who is nothing like you in appearance, age, and attitude.

Again, this is probably another type of book you'd never be caught dead flipping through. (Although, more power to you if it isn't.) So take advantage of the airplane's anonymity and crack into one of these Fabio-covered, lusty page-turners.

628
Pick up a trashy romance novel.

Traveling can be quite the hassle, but a good laugh could make it all better. Pack one of the many collections of Calvin & Hobbes strips in your carry-on and flip through it during turbulence. It will settle your nerves, put a smile on your face, and remind you of the amazing power of a child's imagination.

629
Laugh at Calvin & Hobbes.

You're on an airplane; the book takes place on an airplane. Get it? A great no-brainer for what to bring onboard is a book that centers on an airplane ride. Visit your local bookstore or library and grab a copy of *Sagittarius Rising*; *Red Tail Captured, Red Tail Free*; or *The Hitchhiker's Guide to the Galaxy* (granted, this one takes place on an intergalactic sort of airplane).

630
Read airplane books.

631
Read *The Catcher in the Rye.*

Maybe this has already landed on your list of favorites to reread, or it's one of the literary classics you intend on picking up. However, the reason it's listed specifically is because it's probably a book you've never read at all, but have played it off like you have. So quit fooling around and pick up a copy before your flight. Enjoy the story of young Holden, and if anyone asks you can just say you're rereading one of your favorites.

632
Pick up some Picoult.

A literary hero for the masses of young women who flock to the bookstores, Jodi Picoult has a string of critically cheered and crowd-pleasing titles available. If you're one of the young women who has never dipped into a Picoult novel, rectify that on your next flight. And if you're a guy, give it a chance and grab a copy— you can always slip the dust-jacket for *Ron Jeremy: The Hardest (Working) Man in Showbiz* over it.

633
Get lost in regional literature.

A great way to get acquainted with the area of the country you'll be visiting is by picking up a book or two set in your destination. Headed to the South? Get a feel of its storied past by picking up some Faulkner for your flight. Granted, a lot's changed since the time when his novels were set, but the rich Southern landscape and feel that he captured in his books still resonates.

Before you get onboard, browse the young adult section of the bookstore. See what's receiving top placement in this age-defined genre and pick up a copy of whatever interests you the most. If anything, it will provide some light reading for the plane.

634
What are the kids reading these days?

A lot of bookstores feature books from upcoming authors. Take a look at the various offerings. There's definitely going to be something that piques your interest. And once you've read the book you can pass it along to your friends, claiming that you've discovered this young, talented up-and-comer.

635
Check out the fresh faces of literature.

Many famous writers have butted heads with their peers. There was a little more than just a friendly competition between Hemingway and Faulkner, and Hemingway and Fitzgerald as the three were the top novelists of their time. Pick up a novel from each of these rivals and see who you side with—a good Hemingway choice in this situation may be *A Moveable Feast*, which features his relationship with Fitzgerald.

636
Pick a side between dueling authors.

PRANKS

You're bored. You don't know anyone. And you have plenty of patsies to place the blame on. Why *not* get into a little mischief? Granted, the answers are pretty obvious—a potential black eye, possibly getting restraints, permanent airline bans—but who cares? You only fly once (if you get caught). Live it up and throw back to the days of middle school. You might even lighten up the mood and put a smile on other passengers' faces, or you might get arrested by an air marshal. Your call, just don't blame us.

637
Sneak into first class.

Come on, you know you'd feel better if you knew what it was like up there in those cushy leather seats with all their arm and leg room! Go on up and check it out for yourself. If confronted, fake a foreign accent and complete incomprehension.

638
Leave a message on the mirror.

Before you leave the lavatory, write a message on the mirror with something that's easy to clean off, like lipstick or ChapStick. Go creepy with something like, "I'm watching you!" Or seem ominous with a message of "Beware!" Either way, watch as people exit the bathroom; their faces will be worth the effort. Just be sure to clean the mirror before you deplane—you don't want to be a *real* jerk.

639
Talk to yourself.

Want to really freak out the seatmate next to you? Start mumbling about something completely asinine. When they turn to ask if you were talking to them, give them a blank look and ask what *they're* talking about. Keep going, getting louder and louder each time.

and then answer them! What's stranger than just talking to yourself? Having a full-blown conversation with yourself. Enjoy the looks of panic in the eyes of fellow travelers as you talk to yourself in various voices. Don't say anything that could get you arrested. Just stick to saying things such as "I like pickles. Yes, so do I." After a while, you can tell everyone you're actually quite sane. They may or may not believe you.

640
Ask yourself questions out loud ...

Zess will gut your zeetmays very aye-knowed! So give it a try. Talk about how beautiful France is in the summertime. Try to start a conversation about the croissant. Or go for the ultimate French topic—Jerry Lewis. They can't seem to get enough of this American funnyman.

641
Talk in an exaggerated French accent.

Nobody really looks like the folks in the SkyMall catalog or in-flight magazine. Normal people have scraggly beards and facial blemishes. Here's an idea: Why don't you go through the magazines and give the perfectly coiffed models those blemishes, bad hairdos, and bizarre facial hair? All you're doing is "keeping it real."

642
Deface the in-flight magazines.

643
Fill in all the *o*'s.

If flying scares you, the best thing to do is to take your mind off of the flight. One of the best ways to do this is to begin a repetitive, mind-numbing, pointless, seemingly endless task. Complete the same task you attack during boring business meetings: Fill in all the *o*'s in available reading material. Once you get started, you probably won't even notice minor turbulence.

644
Imitate William Shatner.

A famous *Twilight Zone* episode featured Shatner as a frightened airline traveler. He kept thinking he was seeing something on the wing of the plane, even though no one else could see it. The signature line was "There's (interminable pause) some-thing-on-the-wing" (said as one word). Try the line for yourself and then continue to express your concerns about a 30,000-foot terror to the flight attendant in the same speaking style as Captain Kirk.

645
Practice mime.

Everyone hates a mime. You can emote and bring tears of rage, sorrow, or joy to your seatmates' eyes without saying a word. Pretend there's a wall in front of you. Pretend you are sealed into a box and simply must emerge. Relive the experience of childbirth. See if you can request an extra pillow from the flight attendant by just miming.

Everyone knows the story about the escaped lunatic with a hook for a hand. Everyone also knows that dinosaur-size alligators thrive in the sewers of New York City. The trouble is, neither of these stories is true. They're urban myths, ersatz horror stories utilizing elements of modern life. Make up one of your own, then share it with your seatmates. Eventually, someone else may come up to you and tell you the story that you invented.

646
Launch an urban legend.

Take your time and build up an elaborate story about how you're the best friend of the personal assistant to one of Hollywood's brightest stars. Really make your seatmate believe your relationship with this fictitious person and then drop some sort of slanderous bomb that your friend "revealed" about the star. See if it makes it on any of the gossip blogs or magazines.

647
Start a rumor.

Boarding a plane has got to be one of life's worst mini-epic struggles. Relieve some of that tension by providing some laughs as you walk down the aisle. Slip forward. Slip backward. Slip onto seated passengers. Just be sure to keep a deadpan expression at all times.

648
Practice your pratfalls.

649
Practice armpit farts.

You're never too old to enjoy making farting sounds by placing your hand expertly beneath your underarm while raising and lowering your elbow. See if you can re-create full blasts, church creepers, and all the other delightful sounds of flatulence, right there in your window seat!

650
Get crazy with the Cheez Whiz.

Small cans of aerosol cheese are acceptable on planes, so bring one aboard. Come up with inventive uses for the canned cheese. Squirt some above your top lip and then start a conversation with the person next to you. Or secretly put some in a tissue and then fake sneeze using that Kleenex; then show off your neon orange boogers to your seatmates. Or use it for #638 and scribble a message on the bathroom mirror with it.

651
Talk to the dead.

Let's hope you know that most (read: all) psychics are a croc. However, why not have some fun with any believers that happen to be riding with you? Explain to whoever looks the most gullible that you're a practicing medium and are feeling a strong presence around her. Do your best John Edwards—the ghost whisperer, not the quaffed politician—and channel any spirits who may be hanging around your 747.

Drop something like, "Why did the monkey fall out of the tree?" And then when your fellow passenger has a puzzled look on his face, answer, "It was dead. Get it?!" And then follow up with the loudest, most obnoxious laugh you can muster.

652
Tell dumb jokes.

Start giggling like a schoolgirl whenever someone uses a word that has dirty, alternative meaning like *duty*, *hard*, *but*, or *wood*. It's immature. It's annoying. It's a perfect way to act like a fool.

653
Laugh at suggestive words such as *duty* and *hard*.

Be *that* guy. Shift that seatback to your heart's content without any regard for the person behind you. Move it slightly. Move it as far as it will go. Change positions at least once every three minutes, and see how long it takes to get a swift slap to the back of the head.

654
Constantly adjust your seatback.

655
Throw peanuts and pretend you didn't.

Just because you're a responsible adult doesn't mean you can't act childishly sometimes. Once you get that little pack of peanuts, stash them away until the flight is well underway. Then, from time to time, heave them in different directions. Immediately adopt an innocent pose or feign deep sleep. This can be an especially effective activity on overnight flights, which take place in near-total darkness.

656
Belch the alphabet.

What a fine example of skill and talent. If you're capable of accomplishing such a feat, share its glory with your seatmates. They'll enjoy it—promise! The best bet is to load up on as much soda as humanly possible before you take on this gassy endeavor. You may even get some cheers once you hit Z, but you'll more likely just get hit.

657
Fight for the armrest.

One of the "joys" of flying is the itty-bitty armrest you share with another passenger. You want it for yourself, but your neighbor has already claimed it. Instead of accepting the situation, try slowly and surreptitiously to claim the armrest as your own. If he gets mad, say you're sorry and didn't realize what you were doing. Wait a minute, then start creeping up the side of the armrest again and start this battle all over again.

Bob Dylan once sang a song about "Mr. Jones," an uptight guy trying to make sense of changing cultural times. If you're sitting next to a Mr. Jones, see if you can shake him up a bit. Try to get him to let down his hair. Perhaps you could bring up offbeat topics like your recent sexual escapades or show him your tattoos and piercings.

658
Freak out the squares.

Your mouth is capable of making more sounds than you think. Try all sorts of different things: pops, cracks, whistles, hums. Be creative.

659
Make mouth sounds.

Resurrect your favorite high school prank. Grab a roll of toilet paper from the lavatory and surreptitiously toss it from one end of the plane to the other. The result is a banner of cushy whiteness that trails festively throughout business class.

660
Roll the plane.

661
Start playing a kazoo.

Luckily for the kazoo, listening to nails on a chalkboard is an excruciatingly painful experience. Otherwise this little waxpaper "instrument" would get the rap as the worst sound ever. So take one on the plane and start kazoo-ing "Twinkle, Twinkle, Little Star."

662
Start the wave.

You've seen that guy at the ballpark who tries to corral everyone in the stands to start doing the wave. He's loud, energetic, and gets on your last nerve. Be that guy. Take your seatmates out to the ballgame and go up and down the aisle trying to start the wave. Maybe you'll actually succeed; more than likely you'll end up on the ground in restraints.

663
Snap that bubble wrap.

Come on, admit it. You loved bubble wrap when you were a kid, and you still do. It's a soothing experience for the popper, but not so much for the people around the popping. Stock up on some bubble wrap before you head out on your flight and start popping it once you hit cruising height.

"Ive-gay e-may he-tay eef-bay, ease-play." Throughout the entire flight, speak only in this mutilation of the English language. To speak in pig Latin, simply drop the first consonant or consonant cluster of a word, place it at the end of the word, and add "ay." For example, "bite me" becomes "ite-bay, e-may." You'll probably only be understood by preteens and equally obnoxious folk.

664
Speak only in pig Latin.

It's fun (for you)! And it's sure to get a "conversation" started with the individual in front of you. Don't just kick randomly. Try kicking the rhythm to popular songs, and see if the hapless guy in front of you can figure out which song you're kicking to him.

665
Kick the back of someone's seat.

Go to the lavatory make some hurling sounds and then drop some fake puke into the toilet. Close the lid and head back to your seat. The next one in will find your heinous prank and possibly throw up for real. If you don't happen to have any artificial yak handy, mash up your own concoction at your seat and bring it with you to the restroom. Dump your peanuts, Cheez Whiz, and Diet Coke into the toilet and enjoy.

666
Plant fake barf.

FACE-OFF

It's on! Ali versus Frazier; Johnson versus Bird; Rice versus Sanders; Andre the Giant versus Hulk Hogan; you versus your seatmate. What better way to spend your time than participating in some good ol' fashioned competition? Start up a rivalry with the person sitting next to you and put it to the test with these fun face-off games. Go for the gold as your cabin turns into your stadium and your fellow passengers into cheering fans. Remember, it's only yours to lose.

667
Gross each other out.

Mix condiments and dare one another to eat each other's concoctions—like a mile-high episode of *Fear Factor*. Ask for the ketchup, the mayonnaise, the mustard, the relish, whipped cream, nondairy creamer, and anything else that's available on your flight. Mix together the gross combination. One point for sampling a twisted mixture. Minus a point if you barf upon swallowing. And minus two points if you don't even try it.

668
Have a cracker-eating contest.

You probably did this in Scouts. Take a pack of saltines, stuff them in your face, and see who can swallow the most in the shortest amount of time. Sure, it makes a mess, but someone else has to clean it up, right? So go at it! A variation is to see who can have the most crackers in his mouth and still be able to whistle.

669
Stack it up.

Take on another passenger in a game of stacking. Seem simple and childish? You bet! But it's a fun way of steadying your hand and killing some time. Ask the flight attendant for a more-than-normal amount of creamers. These little sealed cups of coffee creamer are the perfect stacking tool. Drop your tray tables and see how many you can stack on top of each other. Whoever can create the highest tower before it topples wins.

Nothing keeps the mind sharper than coming up with the perfect bon mot, retort, or riposte. It's what the Irish call, "taking the piss out of each other," and is their ultimate sign of friendship. Put friendship aside on this one. Pick a worthy adversary and start firing one-liners at each other. You lose if you crack and call on the flight attendant for a seat change.

670
Trade insults.

Charades is the quintessential icebreaker. Write down some book or song titles on slips of paper. Have seatmates choose a slip and act out whatever's on it. The only real ground rule is that you can't speak. Charades are fun, and they can make the minutes fly by quickly.

671
Play charades.

Resurrect one of your favorite ways to kill time in high school. Fold up a piece of paper into a tight triangle, have a seatmate create ersatz goalposts with her fingers, and try for some field goals.

672
Are you ready for some football?

673
Play goalie.

Table hockey has all the thrills of professional hockey except for time spent in the penalty box. Take two coins and place them a few inches apart at one end of your tray table, and place another two coins a few inches apart at the other end. Wad up a small piece of paper for a puck, and use toothpicks or plastic cutlery for hockey sticks. You'll be amazed at how much time you can waste trying to swat the puck through your opponent's goal.

674
Play quarters.

Could you have survived college without regular competitions of America's favorite drinking game? You remember. All you need to play is a quarter, a cup, and some alcohol. Bounce the quarter off a hard surface. If it lands in the cup, pick a seatmate and make him slam a drink. If you miss the cup, it's someone else's turn.

675
Animal, vegetable, or mineral?

Twenty questions is a timeless game of deductive reasoning that any two or more people can play. It was fun when you were a kid, and it's just as much fun now because your palette of choices is broader. Think of a French Symbolist rather than the fifteen-minutes-of-fame pop idols you chose as a youngster.

All you need is your tray table, two coins, a scoring paper, and a willing competitor. Each of you takes a turn sliding your coin across the tray table with the intent of getting it as close to the edge as possible without dropping off the side. One point if your coin makes it the closest. Two points if it hangs over the edge without falling off. Bumping your competitor's coin off the side with your own is encouraged, so switch up the order every round.

676
Take it to the edge.

It's an oldie, but a goodie. And everyone knows how to play. For a greater challenge, turn the game into an on-the-cheap version of *Hollywood Squares*. Try to stump each other with trivia before placing your X or O.

677
Play tic-tac-toe.

Pick a tongue twister and square off against an opponent in this completely challenging speaking competition. The hardest part will be finding an objective judge to listen to each of you reel off "Sally sells seashells by the seashore." He should judge on clarity, speed, and numbers of recitations.

678
Tongue-twist off.

679

Play hangman.

You remember how to play, right? Draw a makeshift gallows. Think of a phrase. Write blanks corresponding to the letters in the phrase. Ask a seatmate to guess the correct letters. For each right answer, place the letter in the blank. If he or she is wrong, begin to draw a stick figure hanging from the gallows.

680

Pit your fantasy team against your seatmate's.

First, find a willing seatmate. Next, think of a sport. Argue with each other about who gets to be on which team. Then let these two teams go at each other in the ultimate showdown. Who wins? That's up to the two of you to decide. Just don't let things heat up to the point of causing a midair disturbance. Those are particularly unwelcome these days.

681

It's Fingers Twister!

Twister is Hasbro's classic party game during which players contort their bodies and intertwine with one another to put hands and feet on colored circles. Simply create a tiny version of the game's board and create a spinner corresponding to different fingers. Then play against your seatmates.

Clasp hands with someone else, leaving your mutual thumbs free. At the proper signal, try to pin down your seatmate's thumb. That's all there is to the exciting sport of thumb wrestling—but competition can be fierce, as well as addictive.

682
Thumb wrestle.

If you are proud of your forearm's strength, challenge someone else to one of humankind's greatest sports challenges: arm wrestling. Make a friendly wager prior to your epic bout. Perhaps the loser will have to buy drinks for the winner.

683
Arm wrestle.

Even if all you're playing for is quarters, pretzels, or drinks, the game of bingo will still get your heart racing. It combines the thrill of competition with the ease of dumb luck, so bring along some cards and a jar full of pennies to mark the cards. Be sure to scream *"bingo"* extra loudly every time you win.

684
Play bingo.

685
Play Monopoly.

The very thing that makes Monopoly a liability at parties makes it a joy on an airplane: the game monopolizes your time! Vary the rules to change the length of the game. You can determine that whoever has the most money at the end of a half-hour is the winner, or you can double the amount of fines and purchases so that bankruptcy occurs earlier. So whether you're on a two-hour or a transatlantic flight, Monopoly can keep you and your seatmates busy.

686
Play Scrabble.

Scrabble is Hasbro's classic vocabulary game. Players get a number of tiles with letters on them. The object is to spell words on the game board. It's challenging and helps build your vocabulary and critical thinking skills. Play against one other person, or create teams using the folks around you.

687
... Or opt for Upwords.

Upwords is similar to Scrabble, with one important difference: The tiles are stackable. You can create new words by placing new letter tiles on top of old ones to spell new words. The higher you stack the tiles, the higher your score. It adds another dimension to an already challenging game.

Sure, it sounds a little ridiculous, killing brain cells in the name of sport, but it's a whole lot better than just letting them get a free ride wasting away, which will happen if you choose to just zone out during your flight. Break out the watch, match up against a seatmate, and see who can go the oxygen-free distance.

688
Hold your breath.

The meant-for-inside-play Nerf Ball debuted in 1969. Nerf basketballs and basketball hoops have adorned college dorm rooms ever since. Bring the setup along with you on the plane. Ask each other trivia questions. Right answers allow you to take a shot. Play until you reach ten points or twenty points or whatever.

689
Go Nerf.

This game is named after a novel by Jack Dann entitled *The Man Who Melted*. Place an author's name before or after the title of his book in order to make up a funny phrase or sentence. Another example is John Updike's 2002 novel, *See My Face*, which becomes See My Face, John Updike. Give yourself and your competitor five minutes to list as many as you can think of. Whoever has the most originals that didn't repeat on the other's list, wins.

690
Play The Man Who Melted Jack Dann.

691
Have a spoon-off.

Ask the flight attendant for two spoons. On the count of three, both of you place your spoon on the tip of your nose. Whoever can balance his spoon on the end of his nose the longest wins.

692
Play jacks.

You probably haven't tried playing jacks since you were a kid, but that doesn't mean the game isn't still fun. That tray table is a perfect playing field. This children's game actually turns out to be great for developing your hand-eye coordination.

693
Play categories.

Categories is a simple game to play that can be a great time-killer. You can play it by yourself or with others. Come up with a list of categories: state capitals, birds, books, famous artists, and so on. Then choose a letter of the alphabet—say, *R*. Set a two-minute time limit and see how many *R*-words you and your opponent can come up with for each of the categories.

Ghost is a word game you've probably played before. One player begins with a letter. The next player has to add a letter. The next player adds another. The letters must have the potential to spell words. The object is *not* to be the one who completes the word.

694
Play ghost.

Novelist Vladimir Nabokov popularized in *Pale Fire* the word game that has come to be called word golf. The object is to change one word to its opposite by changing one letter at a time. For example, Nabokov's fictional John Shade turns a lass into a male in the following way: lass, mass, Mars, mare, male. Choose a word and see who can change it into its opposite in the fewest number of letter substitutions.

695
Try word golf.

Your library or bookstore will have books of short mysteries that you can solve. If all else fails, go to the children's section and pick up one of those Encyclopedia Brown books you read as a child. The mysteries test your powers of concentration and critical thinking, so they're a great way to boost your brainpower. Read the mystery out loud and whoever can come up with the correct response wins a point. First one to solve five wins the Sherlock-off.

696
Solve some three-minute mysteries.

697
Play Spot the Difference.

This game isn't just for children anymore! Versions for adults have come into vogue in recent years. The basic setup is this: Two pictures sit side by side. At first glance, they appear to be exactly the same. However, if you look closely, you'll see that there are subtle differences between the two pictures. Spot the Difference is a great game to build your powers of observation.

698
Play hide and seek.

First, find a willing seatmate. Then take an object and hide it somewhere between your row and the lavatory. See if he can find the object. Give him hints: "You're getting warmer. No, no ... colder, colder." Once he finds the hidden item, let him hide something from you.

699
Boggle your mind.

Boggle is a simple word game that's eminently portable. To play, simply shake up the game's plastic box, which contains sixteen cubes containing various letters. The object is to create words from the resulting "boggled" letters. The trick is that the letters have to be adjacent to one another. Compete with a seatmate.

One way to boost brainpower is to rearrange the letters within words to form new words. Choose a rather long, multisyllabic word and write it atop two sheets of paper. Set a time limit and see how many words you and your competitor can come up with. Whoever ends up with the most words is the victor, and should be treated to a drink.

700
Scramble some words.

Battleship is an easy and fun game to play that's available in a travel-size version. For the game, you have ships that you place at various spots on a board. Then your opponent tries to guess on which spots your boat sits. There's not a whole lot of opportunity for strategy, but the game is fun. You can make a variation, such as having your opponent take a drink each time you sink one of her ships.

701
Play Battleship.

Pocket-size chess sets are available in most department and toy stores. Pick one up and engage a seatmate in the world's foremost game of wits and strategy. If he doesn't know how to play, you can teach him the fundamentals of chess in a few minutes. But beware of beginner's luck!

702
Checkmate!

703
King me!

Everybody knows how to play checkers. It's *the* classic game of classic games. You can probably find a miniature version of checkers at any toy or department store. Play against fellow passengers for bragging rights.

704
War.

Split a deck of cards between you and your seatmate and then go head-to-head flipping over the top card of your decks. The higher card wins and the winner keeps both cards. If you both throw down the same number or face card, place two cards from the top of your deck on top of the card you just played and then throw the third card down face up. Whoever's is the highest wins all of those cards. Keep going until someone has all the cards.

705
Go fish!

If there are only two of you playing, deal each of you seven cards. If you've found more than one person to join in, deal five cards to everyone. All players then take a turn asking another person if he has a match for a card in their hands. And if he doesn't, go fish! That player grabs a card from the pile and sees if it's a match. If it isn't, it's just another card in their hand.

Deal out ten cards to each player. Make either a *set* (three or four cards sharing the same rank) or a *run* (three or four cards of the same suit in sequence). Take a turn by pulling a card from the stockpile or the discard pile, laying down sets or runs, and then discarding. The round ends when someone discards his last card. Count up the points for each player. Subtract the points from the other players' totals. Keep playing rounds until someone makes it to three hundred.

numbered cards = 5, face cards = 10, aces = 15

706
Spice it up with some rummy.

Ugly carpeting, lots of people, and dim lights—it's like you're at a casino—sort of. Start dealing cards and going for broke with a pickup game of blackjack. The goal is to get to twenty-one, with face cards having a ten-point value and aces working as either eleven or one. Turn your plane ride into a Vegas practice session.

707
Blackjack.

Break out the chips you packed in your carry-on or use coins as chips. Deal two cards to each player. Take bets. Flip the next three cards, which are the "flop," and begin the next round of bets. Next the "turn" card is dealt, and there is another round of bets before the "river" card is flipped by the dealer and players show their hands. Whoever has the best hand wins.

Hierarchy of hands: straight flush; four of a kind; full house—three of one rank, two of another; flush—all the same suit; straight; three of a kind; two pair; a pair; high card

708
Texas hold 'em.

709
Have some five-card fun.

Deal each person a card face down, then go back around and deal everyone one card face up. The person with the highest card starts the betting. Once everyone has a chance to bet or fold, deal a third card face up to everyone. Betting begins with whoever has the best two-card poker hand. Next comes a fourth card face up, and another round of bets. Finally, a fifth card should be dealt face up, any final bets made, and then the first card is flipped over for a showdown.

710
Play Uno.

Uno is a simple card game that anyone can learn to play instantly. You can pick up the special deck of cards almost any-where: department stores, drug stores, maybe even at one of the terminal shops. The object of the game is to be the first to get rid of all seven cards you've been dealt by matching the colors or numbers on a discard pile. You can get a good game started with just one other player, or you can play Uno with several competitors.

711
Play Trivial Pursuit.

Pit your knowledge of trivia against other players' in a hot game of Hasbro's Triv-ial Pursuit. Rather than bring the game board and pieces onto the plane, you can simply bring the cards that contain the questions. Alternate categories and keep score using a pen and paper.

The category on *Jeopardy!* that seems to trip up the majority of contestants is world geography. Get yourself ready to face Alex Trebek. Pick up a world atlas and familiarize yourself with the world's major rivers and mountain ranges. Next category: Game show success!

712
Get ready for *Jeopardy!*

One player draws a card with a word or phrase on it. Without saying anything, he must draw the word or phrase and hope he does it well enough to get his teammates to guess the clue within a prescribed amount of time. It's a great icebreaker for large groups, but you can play it with just three people, and you don't need to purchase the game to play. All you need is some clues, some paper, and a writing implement.

713
Play Pictionary.

IN-CHAIR AEROBICS

You can't use the old standby that the gym's too far away to avoid working out while you're soaring through the sky. In this case, you're already sitting in the gym. Using your body weight and seat, you can give yourself a workout that will leave you refreshed and toned. These isometric exercises may get you a couple of stares from fellow seatmates, but you'll be the one laughing when their legs cramp.

714
Foot rotations.

This easy exercise will keep your toes and feet from cramping, and cut down on those awkward shuffles out of your row and into the aisle to walk off the pins-and-needles feeling. Simply cross your legs at the ankles and rotate your foot ten times clockwise, then ten times counter-clockwise. Switch feet and repeat.

715
Calf raises.

Keep those calves toned and sculpted. Sit straight up in your seat and place your feet on the ground. Plant your toes and raise your heels. Do this twenty-five times. For added resistance, you can place your hands on your knees and push down as you raise your heels.

716
Toe lifts.

Plant both of your heels firmly in that plush airline carpet. Lift your toes up and hold that position for three seconds and then bring your toes back down. Repeat this exercise fifty times. And then reward yourself with some peanuts.

Sit straight back in your seat and rotate your head in a clockwise motion. Keep the rotations slow and the path wide. Once you complete fifty clockwise rotations, stop and begin fifty counterclockwise rotations. It may be best to close your eyes and focus on something else as you move your head, otherwise you may need to use your airsickbag.

717
Head rotations.

Nothing says elegant more than a long, shapely neck. Start with your neck in the upright position, and then bring your chin forward until it meets your chest. Pause there for one second. Then bring your head back slowly until the back of your head touches your shoulders. Pause there for one second, and then bring it back to the resting position. Complete twenty-five of these exercises.

718
Neck stretches.

This will most likely have eyes darting your way, but don't worry about it. Sit back and relax your shoulders. Begin moving both shoulders in unison in a clockwise rotation. Complete thirty full shoulder circles in the clockwise direction, pause, and then begin doing thirty more shoulder circles in the counterclockwise direction. This little exercise helps reduce back tension, and is a great way to warm up for a nap.

719
Shoulder circles.

720
Fist clenches.

Give your hands a real workout. Start with both of your hands as clenched fists, palms up. Release the fists and stretch your fingers as far out as possible—*really* stretch. Hold this stretched position for two seconds and then recoil your fingers back into fists. *Really* clench those fists. Squeeze your fists for two seconds and then outstretch your fingers again. Do this fifty times.

721
Knee lifts.

A great, easy workout to tone up those hard-to-reach lower abs, knee lifts can be done with little hassle. Simply sit straight up, bring your knees together, and raise them in unison. The higher you bring them and the longer you hold them up in the air, the better the workout. Try to hold your feet off the ground for five seconds every lift. Go for the gold and see if you can complete 100 lifts without tiring yourself out.

722
Torso twists.

Turn yourself into a tank. Hold out your arms and bend your elbows slightly. Keep your butt firmly planted in the seat and turn your torso to the right, return to the center, then to the left, and return again to the center. Remain facing forward the whole time. Do thirty complete twists.

Granted, this a little different than the gym, since you don't have any dumbbells—unless you packed some in your carry-on. But weightless biceps curls can have an impact on your arm tone if you do enough of them. Plant your elbow on your armrest and curl your fist up to your shoulder. Make sure the motion is even and slow. Complete twenty-five curls with one arm then switch to the other and do twenty-five more.

723
Biceps curls.

Want an easy way to strengthen your forearm for your next game of badminton? Outstretch your arm with your fingers in a loose fist. Squeeze your fist tightly, hold for five seconds, and then release. Do fifty squeezes with one hand and then switch over and do fifty with the other.

724
Palm squeezes.

Extend one leg out in front of you and reach down with the same side's arm, with the intention of touching that foot's toes. Hold that position for three seconds and then return to your rest position. Do twenty-five of these stretches on one side then switch over to the other and complete twenty-five more. Keep it up and you'll be less likely to pull a hammy the next time you're out on the court.

725
Hamstring stretches.

726
Crossed leg pulls.

This one requires a little bit more room than the others, so apologize in advance to your seatmate for any unintended kicks. Cross one leg over the other at the knee and pull your knee up to your chest. Hold your knee to your chest—or as close as you can bring it—for three seconds. Do this fifteen times and then switch legs, completing another fifteen with the other one.

727
Gluteus squeezes.

Work your ass off—or in this case, work it into a more shapely figure. Whatever you do, don't just sit on it. Well, actually, in this case, you should. Sit straight up and squeeze your gluteus muscles. Hold that position for five seconds. Release and rest for one second, and then squeeze and hold again. Repeat this one hundred times.

728
Body raises.

This may be a little advanced for some, so don't worry if you have to pass on this one. Give your upper body a workout by using your whole body weight as resistance. Ask your seatmate if he doesn't mind your hogging the armrests, then grip both and lift your entire body off of your seat. Hold yourself above the seat for three seconds and then return butt to cushion. Try to complete twenty-five full-body lifts.

STUFF TO PONDER

Now's your chance to just *think*. Your mind is clear, you don't have any of those daily distractions bugging you—it's your time. The hardest thing to do at times is just find a moment for yourself and your thoughts. This plane ride will provide you with plenty. Go through these various prompts and let your mind wander; wonder what you really think about a subject now that you have a moment. Take advantage of this time, as it won't last forever.

729
How can you change the world?

Yes, *you*. From your cramped seat on a plane, think of the ways in which you can positively affect your fellow human. Are you passionate about the environment? Do inner-city struggles make you upset? Does the AIDs epidemic in Africa keep you awake? Whatever the problem, think about how you can help be part of the solution, whether it's through a donation or your volunteering.

730
Who inspires you?

Is there someone in your life who really inspires you? Maybe it was a teacher who believed in your abilities. Perhaps it's a friend who serves as your external conscience. It might even be an author whose work you find particularly galvanizing. Have you ever thanked these folks for being a guiding light in your life? No? What's stopping you? Write to them. Tell them what they have meant to you.

731
How have you been acting recently?

For example, if you've been down lately, take time to consider your recent actions. Are you doing anything new or unusual? Have you faced changes beyond your control? Once you've jotted down an assessment of your actions, determine what—if anything—you can do to change them for the better. Resolve to make those changes. If you're facing circumstances beyond your control, resolve to make peace with and embrace those changes.

Let's say you get safely to your destination, walk out of the airport, and get hit by a taxi. How do you think you would be remembered? Happy with the answer? What could you do—right now—to change the answer? Resolve to put those changes into practice. And if you are happy with the answer, you are very fortunate. What have you done right? It's even more fun to think about that.

732
How would you like to be remembered?

When you were little, you wanted to be a stand-up comic because you thought it would be the greatest job ever. Now that you're all grown up, are you actually a stand-up comic? If not, why not? If so, how does it feel?

733
Are you living your dream?

In 2006, travelers awaiting flights at Chicago's O'Hare Airport saw a mysterious craft in the sky. For a few days, the news was filled with stories of UFOs—unidentified flying objects. Though it's a little disconcerting to debate the existence of aliens while zooming through the air, it's still a fascinating subject. Almost everyone has seen something unusual in the night sky. Do you believe?

734
Is there life in outer space?

735
Is your glass half full or half empty?

Decide whether you are an optimist or a pessimist by describing a glass filled up halfway. If you think it's half empty, you're probably a pessimist. If, on the other hand, you think it's half full, chances are good you're an optimist. So is your glass half empty or half full? Are you happy with your response?

736
What's the weirdest way to die?

You've probably heard plenty of stories of tragically awkward deaths—either as a result of stupidity or chance. But what's the weirdest? Is that the way you would want to go?

737
What recent event has touched your life?

The average lifetime is filled with numerous news events that shake the world and change your life. Some, like 9/11 or the murders at Virginia Tech University, are obvious touchstones. Other stories, while more obscure, may nonetheless have had a great impact on you. Which ones have resonated and made an impact on your life? Why?

You've always wanted to visit Topeka, Kansas, and now you're on your way there! Now that one dream is coming true, where else do you want to go in this wide world of ours? Do you crave excitement or placidity? Beauty or bustle? Think hard about the places you really want to see before you die, and make a resolution to visit all seven before it's too late.

738
Where are seven places you want to visit in your life?

"Desert island discs" has been coined to describe those albums in your collection that are indispensable. They contain the music you'd be satisfied listening to for the rest of your days stranded on a deserted island. Which artists' albums have made a big enough impact on your life to warrant their place in your limited, but infinite rotation?

739
What are your five "desert island discs"?

An infamous commercial once featured a man in a lab coat who claimed not to be a doctor, though he played one on TV. Apparently, this made him a credible pitchman for a pain-relief product. Is there a TV doctor you wouldn't mind wielding a scalpel over you? Perhaps you prefer the curmudgeonly Dr. Gregory House of *House*, *Grey's Anatomy*'s emotional Meredith, or the youthful demeanor of teenage doc Doogie Howser. Who would you trust?

740
Which TV doctor would you trust with your life?

741
Who keeps you tuned in?

Bob Barker! Alex Trebek! Bob Barker! Alex Trebek! It's okay to admit that you are addicted to certain game shows. These types of television shows have been around for a *long* time, so there are quite a few hosts to choose from. Your choice of top television really says something about your personality (humorous, intelligent, pretentious, etc.), so choose wisely.

742
Would you rather be invisible or be able to fly?

A simple psychological test of your superhuman preference can determine the basic bedrock of your personality. If you'd prefer the ability to fly, you're probably adventurous and a risk taker with optimistic attitudes. If you'd opt for invisibility, you're much more of thinker than a quick reactor. Does your answer profile fit your personality?

743
What was the happiest day of your life?

Perhaps it was your wedding day, the day you got a huge promotion, or the day of your first child's birth. It was the happiest day of your life, and you can remember it as if it was yesterday. Why did it make you so happy? Also, see how many details you can recall about that day. You'd be surprised.

You spend so much time on the move—
you're literally flying right now—that
you probably don't take a minute to think
about what's really important to you.
What and who helps you get out of the
bed every morning? Understanding your
motives for being is an important part of
human life. So give yourself a few minutes and decide what motivates you.

744
What makes
you tick?

High school is a time most of us will
never forget, even though we might like
to erase some of its memories from our
consciousness. But take a moment to
think about the best memory of your high
school experience—the day you won the
big game, going to your senior prom, or
acing an extremely difficult final. Revel in
those crazy high school days.

745
What's your
fondest
high school
memory?

On the flip side of the previous entry,
what is the memory that you would *really*
want to erase? Some bad things that happened in high school stick with us to this
day, and still prove to be inhibitions to
our current actions. Can you pinpoint
one? How would its erasure affect your
life today?

746
What was
your worst
high school
experience?

747
What do your dreams mean?

Dreams are a forest of symbols that reveal profound truths about you. If you can decode them, you will find that your subconscious mind is giving you instructions to improve your waking life. Really think about the last dream you had, or any recurring ones that keep coming up. See if you can unravel any hidden meanings on your own. If not, you may want to consult a book on the subject.

PUZZLE ANSWERS

Answers to Anagrammar Puzzles

Anagrammar Puzzle #1: Granite (tearing)

Anagrammar Puzzle #2: Hornet (throne)

Anagrammar Puzzle #3: Yarn (Ryan)

Anagrammar Puzzle #4: Cans (scan)

Anagrammar Puzzle #5: Garden (danger)

Anagrammar Puzzle #6: Design (signed)

Anagrammar Puzzle #7: Eighth (height)

Anagrammar Puzzle #8: Loves (solve)

Anagrammar Puzzle #9: Crooner (coroner)

Anagrammar Puzzle #10: Halls (shall)

Anagrammar Puzzle #11: Fighter (freight)

Anagrammar Puzzle #12: Kyoto (Tokyo)

Anagrammar Puzzle #13: Melon (lemon)

Anagrammar Puzzle #14: Paris (pairs)

Anagrammar Puzzle #15: Note (tone)

Anagrammar Puzzle #16: Fleeing (feeling)

Anagrammar Puzzle #17: Easel (lease)

Anagrammar Puzzle #18: Heads (shade)

Anagrammar Puzzle #19: Peach (cheap)

Anagrammar Puzzle #20: Ring (grin)

Anagrammar Puzzle #21: Meteor (remote)

Anagrammar Puzzle #22: Rockets (restock)

Anagrammar Puzzle #23: Sauces (causes)

Anagrammar Puzzle #24: Cadet (acted)

Anagrammar Puzzle #25: Trees (terse)

Answers to Letter Equation Puzzles

Letter Equation #1: 12 = Months in a Year

Letter Equation #2: 6 = Pockets on a Pool Table

Letter Equation #3: 12 = Men on the Moon

Letter Equation #4: 1 = Peck of Pickled Peppers Peter Piper Picked

Letter Equation #5: 13 = Cards in a Suit

Letter Equation #6: 21 = Dots on a Die

Letter Equation #7: 24 = Letters in the Greek Alphabet

Letter Equation #8: 1,000 = Words a Picture is Worth

Letter Equation #9: 26.2 = Miles in a Marathon

Letter Equation #10: 5 = Rings on the Olympic Flag

Letter Equation #11: 99 = Bottles of Beer on the Wall

Letter Equation #12: 5 = Stars on the Chinese Flag

Letter Equation #13: 100 = Zeros in a Googol

Letter Equation #14: 60 = Miles Per Hour that a Cheetah can Run

Letter Equation #15: 9 = Players on a Baseball Field

Letter Equation #16: 2 = Turtle Doves and a Partridge in a Pear Tree

Letter Equation #17: 88 = Keys on a Piano

Letter Equation #18: 2 = Seats on a Tandem Bicycle

Letter Equation #19: 3 = Little Kittens that Lost Their Mittens

Letter Equation #20: 20 = Fingers and Toes on the Human Body

Letter Equation #21: 1 Chinese Lunar Year = 354 Days

Letter Equation #22: 9 = Squares in Tic-Tac-Toe

Letter Equation #23: 10 = Events in a Decathlon

Letter Equation #24: 3 = Primary Colors in the Color Wheel

Letter Equation #25: 100 = Decades in a Millennium

Letter Equation #26: 23 = Pairs of Chromosomes in the Human Body

Letter Equation #27: 384,400 Kilometers = the Distance to the Moon from the Earth

Letter Equation #28: 2 = Legs in a Pair of Pants

Letter Equation #29: 4 = Quarters in a Whole

Letter Equation #30: 2 = Years between the Summer Olympics and the Winter Olympics

Answers to Pencil Surgery Puzzles

Pencil Surgery Puzzle #1: Pleat & Plea

Pencil Surgery Puzzle #2: 113 & 13

Pencil Surgery Puzzle #3: Drive & Dive

Pencil Surgery Puzzle #4: Glove & Love

Pencil Surgery Puzzle #5: 212 & 21

Pencil Surgery Puzzle #6: Hair & Air

Pencil Surgery Puzzle #7: Land & Lad

Pencil Surgery Puzzle #8: March & Arch

Pencil Surgery Puzzle #9: Stormy & Story

Pencil Surgery Puzzle #10: 1901 & 101 (Dalmations)

Pencil Surgery Puzzle #11: Scold & Cold

Pencil Surgery Puzzle #12: Bride & Ride

Pencil Surgery Puzzle #13: Ship & Hip

Pencil Surgery Puzzle #14: Pine & Pin

Pencil Surgery Puzzle #15: Trip & Tip

Pencil Surgery Puzzle #16: Coast & Cost

Pencil Surgery Puzzle #17: 225 (15 squared) & 25 (5 squared)

Pencil Surgery Puzzle #18: Ground & Round

Pencil Surgery Puzzle #19: 10,080 & 1,000

Pencil Surgery Puzzle #20: Pinto & Pint

Pencil Surgery Puzzle #21: Pinch & Inch

Pencil Surgery Puzzle #22: Sweat & Seat

Pencil Surgery Puzzle #23: Tear & Tea

Pencil Surgery Puzzle #24: Mouse & Muse

Pencil Surgery Puzzle #25: Duet & Due

Pencil Surgery Puzzle #26: Pole & Poe

Pencil Surgery Puzzle #27: 3,000 & 300

Pencil Surgery Puzzle #28: Lawn & Law

Pencil Surgery Puzzle #29: Snail & Nail

Pencil Surgery Puzzle #30: Palace & Place

Pencil Surgery Puzzle #31: Flag & Lag

Pencil Surgery Puzzle #32: Chop & Hop

Pencil Surgery Puzzle #33: Fire & Ire

Pencil Surgery Puzzle #34: Nice & Ice

Pencil Surgery Puzzle #35: Plants & Pants

Pencil Surgery Puzzle #36: Shard & Hard

Answers to Rebus Puzzles

Rebus Puzzle #1: Musical instruments

Rebus Puzzle #2: Just between you and me

Rebus Puzzle #3: Abandon (a band on) ship

Rebus Puzzle #4: Accentuate the positive

Rebus Puzzle #5: Watery grave

Rebus Puzzle #6: *Last of the Mohicans*

Rebus Puzzle #7: Backward glance

Rebus Puzzle #8: Nothing between the ears

Rebus Puzzle #9: Painless operation

Rebus Puzzle #10: Long time no see

Rebus Puzzle #11: One step forward, two steps back

Rebus Puzzle #12: Making a monkey out of him

Rebus Puzzle #13: Close, but no cigar

Rebus Puzzle #14: In between jobs

Rebus Puzzle #15: Put your money where your mouth is

Rebus Puzzle #16: I before E, except after C

Rebus Puzzle #17: Too close for comfort

Rebus Puzzle #18: Space invaders

Rebus Puzzle #19: Wise guy

Rebus Puzzle #20: Foreign currency

Rebus Puzzle #21: Forbidden fruit

Rebus Puzzle #22: Up in smoke

Rebus Puzzle #23: Forget about it

Rebus Puzzle #24: No two ways about it

Rebus Puzzle #25: In complete control

Rebus Puzzle #26: Go out on a limb

Rebus Puzzle #27: A nervous breakdown

Rebus Puzzle #28: You ought to be in pictures

Rebus Puzzle #29: Tennessee

Rebus Puzzle #30: The Seven Seas

Answers to Rhyme Time Puzzles

Rhyme Time Puzzle #1: Slow row

Rhyme Time Puzzle #2: Right night

Rhyme Time Puzzle #3: Hair scare

Rhyme Time Puzzle #4: Coy boy

Rhyme Time Puzzle #5: Hour shower

Rhyme Time Puzzle #6: Lizard wizard

Rhyme Time Puzzle #7: Bizarre guitar

Rhyme Time Puzzle #8: Chief thief

Rhyme Time Puzzle #9: Stupid cupid

Rhyme Time Puzzle #10: Mean queen

Rhyme Time Puzzle #11: Great mate

Rhyme Time Puzzle #12: Cheap beep

Rhyme Time Puzzle #13: Tall hall

Rhyme Time Puzzle #14: Spring sing

Rhyme Time Puzzle #15: Chess mess

Rhyme Time Puzzle #16: Pail sale

Rhyme Time Puzzle #17: Neat street

Rhyme Time Puzzle #18: Tire fire

Rhyme Time Puzzle #19: Prune spoon

Rhyme Time Puzzle #20: Big swig

Rhyme Time Puzzle #21: Pig jig

Rhyme Time Puzzle #22: Dime lime

Rhyme Time Puzzle #23: Fat hat

Rhyme Time Puzzle #24: Stable table

Rhyme Time Puzzle #25: Mute flute

Rhyme Time Puzzle #26: Nice mice

Rhyme Time Puzzle #27: Best guest

Rhyme Time Puzzle #28: Stuck truck

Rhyme Time Puzzle #29: Well-done bun

Rhyme Time Puzzle #30: Sole patrol

Rhyme Time Puzzle #31: Bug slug

Rhyme Time Puzzle #32: Red head

Rhyme Time Puzzle #33: Flint stint

Rhyme Time Puzzle #34: Neck check

Rhyme Time Puzzle #35: Cue you

Rhyme Time Puzzle #36: Bow now

Answers to Odd One Out Puzzles

Odd One Out Puzzle #1: Apple (the rest are contained in the "Twelve Days of Christmas" lyrics)

Odd One Out Puzzle #2: Ketchup (it's the only flavor the Baskin Robbins actually made into an ice cream)

Odd One Out Puzzle #3: California (each of the other states contains a city of the same name)

Odd One Out Puzzle #4: Pale (the others can be properly typed using only your left hand on the keypad)

Odd One Out Puzzle #5: Rome (unlike the others, there's a city named Rome on every continent)

Odd One Out Puzzle #6: Door (the other words use the short vowel sounds)

Odd One Out Puzzle #7: Parrot (the remaining animals were all pets of the Kennedy family when JFK was president)

Odd One Out Puzzle #8: Loyal (the others are all names of car models)

Odd One Out Puzzle #9: Sofa (if you replace the last letter of the other words with *e*, they are still words)

Odd One Out Puzzle #10: Trade (if you remove the *r* from the other words, they still make words)

Odd One Out Puzzle #11: Daniel (the other names have been the most popular baby name for at least one year since 1950)

Odd One Out Puzzle #12: Purple (the other colors are used for street signs)

Odd One Out Puzzle #13: R (the other letters, when written in uppercase, only use straight lines)

Odd One Out Puzzle #14: Giraffe (the other words are symbols in the zodiac)

Odd One Out Puzzle #15: Jealous (the other words are synonyms of one of the dwarves in *Snow White and the Seven Dwarves*)

Odd One Out Puzzle #16: Time (the other words are contained in the bagua symbol of feng shui)

Odd One Out Puzzle #17: Teddy (the other words are in the lyrics of "Santa Claus Is Coming to Town"

Odd One Out Puzzle #18: Romeo (Romeo is the only one who is not a Shakespearean king)

Odd One Out Puzzle #19: Apple (the others were all included in the names of the original Crayola box of 64 crayons)

Odd One Out Puzzle #20: Elephant (the other animals are all part of the Chinese zodiac)

Odd One Out Puzzle #21: Sofa (if you place *The* in front of the others, it's a story name in *Grimm's Complete Fairy Tales*)

Odd One Out Puzzle #22: Jasper (the others are names of the brightest stars seen from Earth)

Odd One Out Puzzle #23: Energy (the remaining words are all flavors of teabags offered by Tazo Tea)

Odd One Out Puzzle #24: Ohio (the rest are members of the top five states with the highest population)

Odd One Out Puzzle #25: New York (the rest are members of the top five states in the United States with largest area)

Odd One Out Puzzle #26: Florida (the remaining states contain cities within the top five highest populations)

Odd One Out Puzzle #27: Tim (the others are names of characters played by Humphrey Bogart)

Odd One Out Puzzle #28: Toronto (the other cities have hosted the Olympics)

Odd One Out Puzzle #29: Switzerland (the rest are all members of North Atlantic Treaty Organization)

Odd One Out Puzzle #30: *The Great Gatsby* (Francis Ford Coppola directed the rest of the movies)

Odd One Out Puzzle #31: Dance (the others are all names of NBA teams)

Odd One Out Puzzle #32: Eyeglasses (the others are titles of Stephen King short stories)

Odd One Out Puzzle #33: Pirate (the rest are all names of National Parks)

Odd One Out Puzzle #34: Chrysler (the others have all made the *Fortune* 100)

Odd One Out Puzzle #35: Kite (if you add an *s* to the beginning and end of the others, they form new words)

Odd One Out Puzzle #36: Poor (the rest spell words when written backward)

Odd One Out Puzzle #37: Crime (the others are auto-antonyms—single words that have meanings that contradict each other)

Odd One Out Puzzle #38: Condors (the rest are names of NFL teams)

Odd One Out Puzzle #39: Choir (the others are names of literary works by Edgar Allen Poe)

Odd One Out Puzzle #40: Humphead wrasse (the other endangered species have been released back into the wild)

Odd One Out Puzzle #41: Sing (the others have homonyms)

Odd One Out Puzzle #42: Bulb (the remaining words are eponyms—words derived from people's names)

Odd One Out Puzzle #43: Display (the others are homographs—words that are spelled the same but have different meanings)

Odd One Out Puzzle #44: Travel (the others are names of Kentucky Derby winners)

Odd One Out Puzzle #45: Hudson (the others are NASA space missions)

Odd One Out Puzzle #46: Cat (the domestic cat is the only one that didn't make an appearance in the Bible)

Odd One Out Puzzle #47: Skip (the others can be made into new words by adding the suffix *ful*)

Odd One Out Puzzle #48: Treasure (the rest are all Rudyard Kipling poem titles)

Odd One Out Puzzle #49: Key (the others are used in various superstitions)

Odd One Out Puzzle #50: Ireland (the others are all in the same time zone)

Odd One Out Puzzle #51: Planet (the other objects are included in at least one of the United States' state flags)

Odd One Out Puzzle #52: Cake (the others are made up of one or more of the first and last letters of a state)

Odd One Out Puzzle #53: Taste (the others are the names of the original nine Ty Beanie Babies)

Odd One Out Puzzle #54: Double (the rest are terms used by winemakers as they weigh and measure wine)

Odd One Out Puzzle #55: Castle (the other words are names of tarot cards)

Odd One Out Puzzle #56: Beach (the rest are titles of Woody Allen movies)

Odd One Out Puzzle #57: Tall (the others are noncomparative adjectives)

Odd One Out Puzzle #58: Goods (the others all end in *s* but are treated like a singular noun)

Odd One Out Puzzle #59: Silver (it's the only word in the list that does not have a rhyming word)

Odd One Out Puzzle #60: Chair (the other words can be combined into anagrams of sports— boot + fall = football; sin + net = tennis; and balk + stable = basketball)